Windmills of Yorkshire

Roy Gregory & Laurence Turner

Little Smeaton

Text © Roy Gregory & Laurence Turner, 2009.
First published in the United Kingdom, 2009,
by Stenlake Publishing Ltd.
54–58 Mill Square, Catrine,
Ayrshire, KA5 6RD

Telephone: 01290 551122
www.stenlake.co.uk
enquiries@stenlake.co.uk

ISBN 9781840334753

Introduction

Yorkshire is a big county. Inevitably its topography varies enormously, which has affected the siting and use of wind power. Running more or less centrally north to south lies the Vale of York, comprising rich farmland and the historic city of York. To the west the county includes a large part of the Pennine Hills, from which streams and rivers flow eastwards into this Vale, through the majestic Yorkshire Dales. Here hill farming is the traditional way of life, but during the eighteenth century the abundant supply of water power attracted the early woollen manufacturers who were seeking water power to drive their new mechanised looms. Ultimately this industry concentrated on the then new and now major towns of Leeds, Bradford, Halifax and others. Further still to the south, the water power sites on the rivers around Sheffield enabled the world-famous Sheffield steel industry to flourish.

To the east of the Vale of York, two quite different areas, bordering on the North Sea, are separated by the Vale of Pickering. To the north lie the North Yorkshire Moors, also a hilly area but where water power is less readily available. The principal urban centre in this area is Middlesborough, which rose to prominence through the production of iron and steel, using ironstone mined on the Moors.

To the south of the Vale of Pickering is the comparatively flat area of the Wolds and the Holderness Plain, where water power is sparse and variable. Its southern border is the Humber Estuary where we find some of the country's leading ports, particularly Kingston-upon-Hull. Here merchants had to rely heavily on wind power before reliable steam engines became available.

Watermills were introduced into Britain by the Romans and by the time of the Domesday Survey (1086) there were approximately 100 watermills in Yorkshire serving an estimated population of 30,000 inhabitants. The watermills were obviously sited along the rivers, mainly in the low-lying areas, but along the chalk Wolds bordering the Holderness Plain water power was all but non-existent. The origin of the windmill in Europe is still an unresolved issue, but what is accepted by reliable authors is that the first firm record of a windmill in the United Kingdom is dated 1185 and relates to the former village of Weedley, which stood at the southern tip of the Wolds overlooking the Humber estuary and near the present village of South Cave. Another 12th century reference occurs at East Coatham, a small village on the coast at the mouth of the River Tees. Such was the need for extra power, or power in areas where there was no water power, that during the 13th century a large number of windmills appeared alongside the Tees Estuary, in the Vales of Pickering and York (as far as Wakefield), and on the Wolds and the Holderness Plain.

A few of the medieval windmill sites have been excavated (some accidentally whilst looking for other things) and the evidence shows that, from the 14th century at least, the windmills in Yorkshire were post mills. The best reported excavation is of a site at Bridlington, where the foundations of two mills dating from the 16th century have been found.

This book attempts to explain the history and significance of the windmill in Yorkshire by reference to illustrations, particularly photographs. This presents a problem in that not every windmill that existed during the 18th and 19th centuries has been photographed. Also, in some cases the windmill is not the central feature of the photograph, so details are not always as clear as one might wish.

Terminology

Technical words and phrases have been kept to a minimum but, for the benefit of readers who are new to this subject, an explanation follows of those words and phrases which it has been necessary to use.

Windmills are grouped into two types - post mills and tower mills. The post mill comprises a timber structure, something like a large shed, called the buck, in which all the milling machinery is contained and on which the sails are mounted. The buck is mounted on a substantial upright post and can be rotated around the post to keep the sails facing into wind. The post is supported by quarter bars (usually four), the upper ends of which are mortised into the post immediately below the floor of the buck. The lower end of the post is located at the centre of two intersecting cross trees, the outer ends of which rest on brick piers. The weight of the buck does not rest on the point at which the cross trees intersect, but rather it is carried by the quarter bars to the outer end of each cross tree and thus to the piers on which the cross trees rest. The function of the cross trees is to stop the quarter bars spreading outwards and also to keep the main post upright (i.e. to stop it rocking). The post, quarter bars and cross trees are referred to collectively as the trestle.

The trestle may be left open to the elements, in which case it is described as an open-trestle mill. By the start of the eighteenth century, it was becoming common to enclose the trestle in a circular brick wall so the enclosed area could be roofed over. The structure thus created is known as the roundhouse which provides both protection for the trestle from the weather and also extra storage space for the miller.

A variant of the post mill is the hollow-post mill, in which the post has a hole drilled down its centre to take a drive shaft to machinery located below the trestle.

The tower mill is a more stable structure. The machinery is installed in the body of the tower, built of either brick or stone, apart from the sails which are mounted on top of the tower on a timber framed cap. To keep the sails facing into the wind it is only necessary to rotate the cap. A version of the tower mill is the smock mill. Mechanically it functions exactly as a tower mill, the difference being that the structure is built of timber.

As to the construction of sails to catch the wind, the earliest design of sail, the common sail, comprises a lattice framework over which a rectangular piece of canvas is spread. The canvas on each sail must be spread individually by hand at the start of each milling session and similarly taken off when milling has finished for the day. It is possible (and necessary!) as wind speed increases to reef the sail by tying part of the canvas out of the wind, but the mill has to be at rest whilst this is done. This is a very arduous part of a miller's work.

Substantial improvements have been made to the mill sail to make the life of the miller less stressful. In 1772 Andrew Meikle, a Scottish millwright, produced the spring sail. He replaced the canvas sail cloth with a series of hinged shutters, usually likened to a Venetian blind, which are connected by cranks to a bar running down the sail. Each bar is connected to a handle at the tip of the sail, held in position by a spring. At the start of the day the miller sets the shutters by adjusting the handle. Once the mill is set in motion, if the wind speed increases the spring allows the shutters to open, spilling wind, and closes them again if the wind speed decreases, thus maintaining a relatively constant speed. However, spring sails still have to be set individually by hand with the mill at rest.

An important improvement appeared in 1789 when Captain Stephen Hooper patented the roller sail. Here the shutters are replaced by small roller blinds, with a piece of webbing attached to the bottom of each blind which is wrapped round the roller below it. Each sail has two bars, one down each side of the sail frame, connected by a linkage to a rod (the striking rod) which passes through the centre of the shaft on which the sails are mounted (the windshaft). At the rear of the striking rod, a wheel (the chain wheel) can be rotated by a chain (the striking chain) which hangs at the rear of the mill. The striking rod, chain wheel and striking chain are collectively called the striking gear. This arrangement provides a significant improvement to the working life of the miller, as all the sails can be set at once and it is not necessary to bring the mill to rest to adjust the sails. There is one drawback in that the sails are not self-acting as is the Meikle spring sail, but this problem can be dealt with to some extent by installing a governor.

The final improvement came in 1807 when William Cubitt combined the shutters of the spring sail and the striking gear of the roller sail, to produce what is today referred to as the patent sail. In Yorkshire it is usual with patent sails for the chain wheel to be replaced by a striking lever which pushes the striking rod backwards and forwards through the windshaft rather than rotating the striking rod as is the case with roller sails. The patent sail is a major benefit to millers as the adjustment of the sails in reaction to changing wind speeds becomes automatic.

Another technical matter concerns the way in which the sails are kept into wind. In the case of the post mill, a stout pole (the tail pole) extending at the rear is used by the miller to rotate the whole body of the mill into the required position. This system is applied to the early tower mills, with the tailpole being fixed to the cap frame. Because of the extra length, in these cases the tail pole usually has triangular bracing. Sometimes a winch is fixed to the end of the tailpole, with a chain wrapped around it which can be attached to bollards placed around the mill.

The fantail, patented by Edmund Lee in 1745, became common on tower mills in the 1770s, in which form it comprised a small windmill at the rear of the cap, set at right angles to the main sails. A linkage connects the fan to a cogged cast iron ring (the curb ring) set on the top of the tower. When the wind is blowing directly at the main sails, it exerts an equal force on each side of the fan, which remains stationary. If the wind changes direction, the extra pressure on one side of the fan causes it to rotate, activating the gears connected to the curb ring. This turns the cap round until the sails are again facing directly into wind. The fantail can also be added to a post mill, usually on a frame at the base of the steps by which the miller gains access to the buck. In such cases the tail pole is removed. The fantail eases the life of the miller yet further.

A less expensive arrangement was derived from the fantail, namely the winding wheel. With this the tower has a curb ring as with the fantail but the fan and its framework are replaced by a wheel over which a chain hangs down to a convenient height, by which the miller can turn the mill to wind manually.

Of the internal machinery, the millstones are the most important. The oldest millstones used in English windmills were extracted from the gritstone quarries above Hathersage in the Peak District, and are called Peak stones by reference to their origin or grey stones referring to their colour. There were other quarries which produced similar stones but these are comparatively rare. The second type of stone was a volcanic lava, quarried near to and imported from Cologne, and are called cullin stones, referring to their origin or blue stones by reference to their colour. Because of the nature of lava (i.e. full of tiny gas bubbles), the surface of the stone produces a good grinding action. Cullin or blue stones were preferred during the eighteenth century for grinding wheat. From at least the end of the eighteenth century, millstones quarried at La Ferté sous Jouarre near Paris became the prime stone for grinding wheat, as it peeled off the bran in such a way as to make it easier to dress out the bran to produce white flour. Such stone used in England was quarried in pieces, usually no more than twelve inches square (0.3m²), and brought to England as ballast, then cut to shape, cemented together and bound with iron bands. These are referred to as French or burr stones.

Other items of equipment were used, mainly sieves of one type or another, viz. the bolter and wire machine for dressing out bran, and a cleaner for preparing the grain for milling.

Little Smeaton

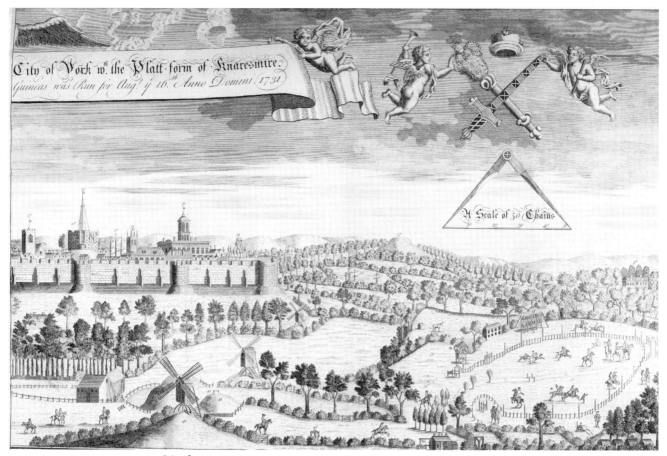

York

Above: Generally speaking each village would have its own mill, either wind or water. The larger towns and cities would need more than one, sometimes a combination of both, and in such built-up areas, the windmills inevitably would be sited on the open ground outside the town. This was the case in York; a *South West Prospect* by John Haynes dated 1731 shows three post mills to the west, not far from the racecourse.

Hull

Right: A plan of Hull published in about 1530, which claims to be a copy of an ancient plan of the town in the British Museum, shows three windmills outside the Beverley Gate to the west of the town, a similar location to those outside York. The area was later known as Myton, which may translate as *milne area* or something similar, and was the site of the town's corn mills until the mid to late eighteenth century.

POST MILLS

Withernwick

NGR SE 196 406

There has been a windmill in the manor since 1304. A "new" windmill referred to in 1612, may date from 1610 when the manor was sold by the Crown to Edward Ferrers and Francis Phillips. The photograph probably shows the windmill very much as it was in 1610, a very basic post mill with an open trestle. In its final days the mill still had common sails. The photograph shows that the stocks (which held the sails) were mounted in a cast iron box (poll end) at the end of the wind shaft. Originally the windshaft would have been made entirely of timber and the stocks mortised into the outer end. This was a weak part of the windshaft and during the third quarter of the eighteenth century it became common to insert a cast iron replacement. The mill continued to operate until the 1890s and was subsequently demolished.

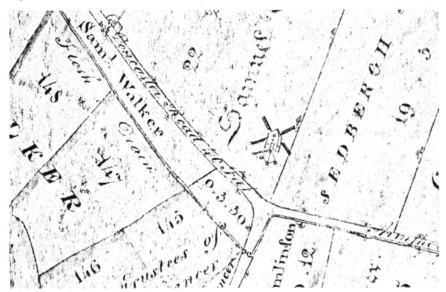

Barnby Dun

NGR SE 620 087

This very small drawing of Barnby Dun Mill, sited in what later became Station Road, is from the Enclosure Award map of 1805. It shows a post mill, with sails, window, ladder and quarterbars, which could well have been the appearance of the post mill. In 1943 it was noted that a ring fence of eighty feet (24m) in diameter marked the site. From the 1840s this mill was replaced by a second one, off Hatfield Lane, but this was demolished many years ago and no more is known apart from the names of the millers up to 1881.

Anlaby

NGR TA 021 289

Another example of an open trestle post mill, which shows quite clearly the normal arrangement of the trestle. There are small struts near the base of the post which appear to be additional quarter bars but this is not so. These extra struts were probably added when the foot of the post started to rot and were simply to reinforce the task of keeping the post upright. Anlaby Mill was probably built during the late 17th century and continued in operation until 1905, being demolished four years later. The mill is similar in design to that at Withernwick except that the sails were attached to a cast iron cross, a device introduced by the famous engineer, John Smeaton, who first used it in 1754/1755 on a windmill at Wakefield.

Little Smeaton
NGR SE 521 170

The open trestle mill at Little Smeaton possessed a fine inscription carved on its post, within the buck, which read -

I x R
J S R
1750

As seen in the photograph, the construction of the buck follows the older millwrighting tradition with no horizontal beams at the end of its crown tree (the cross timber in the buck which rests on the top of the post) but instead, vertical timbers which took some of the weight. There were two pairs of millstones, one at the head and the other at the tail, each turned by clasp-arm wheels mounted on a wooden windshaft. In latter days an engine operated a further pair of stones on the lowest floor of the buck.

George Morritt worked the mill for a number of years until he built a steam mill in the village in 1888. Frederick Shaw worked it intermittently afterwards, but always resisted proposals for its preservation. The windmill's remnants were eventually dismantled and put into storage as late as 1961, with the intention that they should be rebuilt, but the woodwork was then destroyed by fire, and the mill is now only a distant memory.

Swinefleet

NGR SE 777 226

Below: Swinefleet Mill, which stood on the road from Swinefleet to Reedness, was in existence by 1770, and was probably built well before this date, having regard to its small size. The open construction reveals one of the area's remarkable features, in that the post mill has six quarterbars and therefore three crosstrees. This is a rare form of construction, there being only nine examples known in Britain, of which three were in Yorkshire.

The photograph shows Thomas Gringley, the miller, standing in the doorway. His brother John owned the tower mill in Swinefleet at the same time. The post mill was demolished about 1906.

Hemingbrough

NGR SE 675 301

Above: In existence before 1770, Hemingbrough Mill is an example of a Yorkshire post mill which has been modernised. One pair of the common sails has been replaced by a pair of spring sails. The mill was demolished in 1929.

North Anston

NGR SK 525 848

Right: North Anston Mill stood on the east side of the road from Dinnington to the present-day Windermere Court, and the date of 1720 carved on one of the beams gives an indication of the date it was built. This was another example of a Yorkshire post mill with six quarterbars and three crosstrees (see Swinefleet), but these cannot be seen in the photograph, due to an important feature in the development of the post mill. The mill was most likely built as an open trestle mill but, as was common throughout the country, during the early 19th century, the trestle was enclosed in a roundhouse. In most parts of England the conical roof is attached to the circular wall with the apex of the roof being underneath the buck, as was the case here, but this was not the usual arrangement in Yorkshire. The mill was demolished sometime between 1930 and 1939.

Moor Monkton

NGR SE 514 554

Left: The mill standing in 1840 on this ancient site was severely damaged by a dramatic lightning strike, although fortunately the tenant miller at the time, Mr Hopps, was uninjured. This incident provided the opportunity to rebuild the mill to an up-to-date design, with the typical Yorkshire-style roundhouse. In most parts of England the roof was attached to the circular wall of the roundhouse, but in the case of post mills in the Midlands and the North East, the roof was attached to the buck and rotated with it. In Yorkshire there was one further variant which distinguished it from other Midlands-style versions, in that the pitch of the roof was considerably steeper than elsewhere. However, in one aspect this mill was different from most of the post mills in Yorkshire in that the roundhouse was two storeys high, which gave the mill a rather noble appearance. The photograph taken about 1900 shows it going derelict. The roundhouse survived at least until 1942.

Aldbrough

NGR TA 242 390

Below: Probably a late 17th century mill, built originally as an open trestle post mill, but during the early 19th century the trestle was enclosed in a typical Yorkshire roundhouse. At some date the common sails have been replaced by a full set of patent sails. The mill was demolished many years ago.

Thorne, Bellwood's Mill

NGR SE 683 138

Another example of a post mill with a Yorkshire roundhouse, but built of stone not brick as was common elsewhere in the county. The weatherboarding was wider than normal and the entrance door had a canopied porch, a rare piece of adornment on a Yorkshire post mill.

During the nineteenth century no less than seven windmills existed in Thorne, six of which were along the ridge of what is now North Eastern Road and St Nicholas' Road. A seventh stood in Southfield Road. This picture shows the last post mill to survive in Thorne, at the corner of Brooke Street. The last miller was John Bellwood, who worked it with two pairs of millstones and a wire dresser until about 1908, after which it was demolished.

Ferriby

NGR SE 993 273

A typical East Yorkshire post mill with a roundhouse, Ferriby Mill illustrates the next stage in the evolution of the sails, the roller reefing sails patented by Hooper in 1789. The roller sail had two drawbacks. It was not self-regulating without the aid of a governor and the canvas on the rollers was prone to damage in adverse weather conditions. Nevertheless, the roller sail became very popular in parts of Yorkshire, being promoted extensively by millwrights and licensees Norman and Smithson, who had their workshop in Hull. In the photograph the wheel over which the striking chain hangs can be seen on the rear corner of the buck. The mill was demolished in the 1870s.

Wetwang

NGR SE 928 591

Wetwang Mill is another example of an open-trestle post mill having a roundhouse added. The mill illustrates the final stage in the development of the sail used in Britain, Cubitt's patent sail. When patent sails were added to a post mill the striking chain was usually looped over a wheel, as at Ferriby, but at Wetwang the chain was attached to a striking lever, the system generally used when patent sails were installed on tower mills. Using this system, the chain hung further away from the mill body, so in this case the miller built a neat little platform at the rear to enable him to reach the chain. The use of this method of controlling the patent sails, together with the shape of the roundhouse, which is reminiscent of the batter of a tower mill, perhaps suggests the alteration was carried out by a millwright or carpenter who had experience of working on tower mills. The mill was last used in the 1920s, but was demolished shortly afterwards.

Ganstead

NGR TA 152 348

This mill illustrates another arrangement. The mill had been fitted with one pair of roller sails and one pair of spring sails. It is not unusual to find two different pairs of sails on mills in the late 18th century. Given that at the start of the 19th century the sails would be common sails, when spring sails became available after 1772, as an economy measure the miller might partially modernise his mill by changing just one pair of commons for one pair of springs. This would have some benefit as the spring sails were not as powerful as common sails, so changing just one pair would give the miller a degree of self-regulation but also retain a little extra power. If he subsequently changed the other pair of common sails for a pair of roller sails, he might, as an economy, retain the fairly new spring sails. The mill was demolished in 1909.

Stainforth

NGR SE 635 114

By 1750 there were two windmills in Stainforth. A tower mill in the region of Church Road was last noticed in 1893, but its post mill partner, on the north side of the road to Barnby Dun, continued to work as late as 1917. A steam engine helped out in its latter years. Three generations of Harrisons, John, George and Thomas, worked it until 1910, and William Clark took it to the end of its working days. It was gone by 1921, after at least 160 years of labour.

The mill was particularly primitive in its appearance with a tiny gable-roofed buck, set on steep quarter bars and cross trees with supporting brick piers. The sails shown in the photograph again illustrate the mixing and matching of sails, having one pair of roller sails and one pair of spring sails.

Catwick

NGR TA 139 460

Catwick Mill, built as a basic open trestle post mill, clearly underwent a number of changes. What might be described as an economy version of a roundhouse was added, which can have done little more than protect the trestle from weather damage, but it was fitted with the ubiquitous patent sails. An interesting feature of this mill was the extension built on to the rear, probably to provide space for a bolter. Note also there were barely any windows, no porch around the door and no ornamental carpentry. The Yorkshire post mill was a truly functional industrial building. This mill was demolished in 1911.

Brayton

NGR SE 609 313

Above: Brayton had two mills during the nineteenth century and this photograph shows the post mill, located at the end of Long Mann Hills Road, as it stood in 1880. It was still at work by wind alone in 1897, but the end came only six years later, signalling its complete demise soon after. The mill was another example of a Yorkshire post mill with six quarter bars and three cross trees. A boarded half-roof took the place of a properly constructed roundhouse, an even more economic construction than that at Catwick Mill.

Skirlaugh

NGR TA 140 394

Left: The post mill at Skirlaugh was not demolished until 1944 although milling had ceased in 1909. This photograph illustrates the plight of small country millers, who in the latter part of the nineteenth century were fighting to survive in the face of competition from the large roller mills using imported high protein wheat. Here it appears that the original horizontal overlapping weather boarding had rotted and required replacement, but in an attempt to save money the miller has simply covered the existing weather boarding with vertical butted boards. This would have been false economy as water lodging between the two layers of boarding would have exacerbated the original problem.

Beverley Westwood, Fishwick's Mill
NGR TA 027 393

Beverley Westwood, part of some 1,000 acres of common land around the town which in the mid nineteenth century boasted six windmills either on it or immediately adjacent to it, saw the disappearance of some of its mills in unfortunate circumstances. One was Fishwick's Mill, built in 1761 on a small part of the common under a lease for 99 years granted by the Corporation (in fact it was a part of the Westwood which had been set aside for archery practice in the time of Henry VIII). In 1861 the lease expired and the tenant (Fishwick) demolished the mill as required by the terms of the lease, but left the millhouse standing.

During the period of the lease, a bitter dispute arose between the Corporation and the Freemen as to who owned the common land. Thus when the Corporation re-took possession, many of the Freemen objected and there were serious riots in the town. Matters came to a head at 8pm on the 2nd September 1861, when a mob assembled outside the premises but found the gates guarded by two policemen. In the words of the *Beverley Guardian*, the ring leader demanded admittance but upon being refused, "... he retreated a few feet, then sprang over the gate. Thereupon the remainder of the assemblage stormed the gates and gained admittance". The police were clearly outnumbered and, as the report continues, "... this officer, though an old soldier, decided discretion was the better part of valour and beat a hasty retreat". Thereafter the mob burned the house down and removed all vestiges of the mill, including the mound on which the post mill had stood.

Atwick
NGR TA 193 498

This mill was situated to the east of the road north of Hornsea, on the headland overlooking the North Sea. By the late nineteenth century it was fitted with patent sails and had two pairs of millstones, one pair French and the other pair grey. During most of the nineteenth century it was owned by members of the Bell family and following its sale by Robert Bell in 1896 it seems to have gone out of business. The mill was demolished around the time of the First World War.

Snaith, East Cowick Mill
NGR SE 665 214

The mill at East Cowick was quite unlike any other in Yorkshire. It looks from the photograph as though it had an excessively tall roundhouse with a conventional post mill buck perched on top. The lower part of the old brick roundhouse still exists and contains two crosstrees at the conventional level. The roundhouse was raised at some time so that the post became redundant and instead a curb was no doubt fitted around the top of the roundhouse wall, on which the buck was supported, to become very much a proto-tower mill structure. The similarity to a tower mill is even more marked when one considers the method of turning the sails to wind. There was no tailpole and it is most likely that the curb which supported the buck would have been cogged, with a chain wheel installed to enable the miller to wind the mill. Access to the three pairs of millstones was gained internally, since there were no steps as one finds on a normal post mill. The mill is noted for the first time in 1817 and continued to work until a little while after 1908. The structure was taken down in 1917, apart from the roundhouse, which survives as the only remains of a post mill in Yorkshire.

Fockerby
NGR SE 845 201

Down the centuries, windmills have attracted their own folklore. The ardent mill enthusiast, H E S Simmons, discovered a fascinating and mysterious story relating to the mill at Fockerby. Many years ago, it is said, a sailor courted the miller's daughter and the miller objected. One night, when the sailor was on his way to visit the daughter, the miller locked her in the mill and waylaid the sailor. There was a fight during which the sailor was either stabbed or shot, but the miller's dog fought furiously on the side of the sailor, and legend has it that on certain nights this dog is still encountered in the vicinity of the mill. A year or two before 1900 (by which date the mill was a lonely ruin) Mr Lefley of Reedness, another mill enthusiast, was cycling towards the mill when a black shadowy form came up alongside and kept pace with him. In the light of his lamp he could see it was a black retriever. Fear overtook him and in his own words he "rode like the devil" but the dog kept pace with him. As he passed the mill, the dog vanished! Is a ghostly dog ever seen nowadays to run alongside at night along the Garthorpe Road?

EARLY TOWER MILLS

Upton
NGR SE 474 139

Post mills have always been vulnerable to storm damage and as early as 1294 an alternative design, the tower mill, was introduced at Dover Castle. This type of windmill comprised a stone tower with a timber cap on which the sails were mounted and which could be rotated to keep the sails facing into the wind. A characteristic feature of these early tower mills was the cylindrical shape of the tower, the sides being vertical, a form which would be familiar to castle builders. It is not clear how many of these cylindrical tower mills were built, but they were more expensive to build than a post mill and so they were probably quite rare. The earliest survival may be the stone structure at Burton Dassett in Warwickshire (possibly before 1367) but the earliest known example in Yorkshire is not recorded until sometime later, at Pontefract. A seventeenth century description tells of three storeys with the lowest one covered by a mound, the total height of the tower being 24ft.

An early Yorkshire stone tower mill, but with slightly sloping walls 22ft in height and with an external diameter of the base of 22ft stands on Beacon Hill at Upton. The tower comprises three storeys and illustrates the basic arrangement of a tower mill. When sacks of grain enter the mill, they are raised to the top floor by a hoist powered by the sails. From here the grain falls by gravity into the millstones, which are on the middle floor. After passing through the stones, the resultant flour falls, again by gravity, to the lower floor where it is bagged up ready for collection by, or delivery to, customers. The tower mill at Upton may have been used as a house as early as the late eighteenth century, but was condemned for residential purposes in 1903. Now it is simply used as a store.

Askham Richard
NGR SE 542 472

John Ogilby's scrolls of road sections of 1675 show a windmill near the York road at Askham Richard and one at Askham Bryan. The small tower at Askham Richard, standing on a small mound, hides behind a grove of Scotch pines and surely must be that very mill, in which case this mill is an extremely early example of a conical or battered tower mill in Britain. Two pairs of large millstones were once to be seen here. At the end of the nineteenth century the structure was converted to a water tower with a header tank on its top.

Selby, Soke Mill
NGR SE 615 326

In 1760 two watermills on the Mill Dam stream leading to the River Ouse were demolished and replaced by one combined building including both a windmill and a watermill. This print of 1800 shows the windmill (there is no sign of the watermill) as a conical tower mill with a boat shaped cap, four common sails and a horizontal fantail. If the fantail was fitted when the mill was built in 1760, it would be a very early example of this device. The photograph below was taken in 1884 when the tower had been rebuilt. It was demolished only two years later.

Hull, Humber Bank Mill
NGR TA 097 281

During the late medieval period the low lying areas of Holland were being drained to provide good agricultural land. As a result, there was considerable incentive to develop the windmill. By the end of the seventeenth century, the wooden post mill had evolved via the smock mill, into the tall brick conical tower mill. English merchants, carrying out their businesses in the east coast ports, had regular contact with their counterparts in Northern Europe, particularly Holland, and these entrepreneurs were quick to recognise the value of this improved power source. One such was Joseph Pease, an oil miller with three mills in Hull in the early eighteenth century.

In 1747 he decided to concentrate his activities in Wincolmlee and invited a millwright from Rotterdam to build him a new mill in accordance with the latest Dutch practice. By 1750 the mill had been built, comprising a very tall brick tower mill, with a wide braced stage to give access to the sails and tailpole. Within a short space of time, the corn millers started to adopt these new concepts. Humber Bank Mill, dating from 1770, shows clearly the Dutch influence. Apart from the tower itself, there is the tailpole at the rear and the wide braced stage which was necessary to enable the miller to reach the tailpole and the common sails. Both these features can still be seen on many windmills in Holland today. The mill had been demolished by 1791.

Ulleskelf
NGR SE 519 390

By tradition the mill at Ulleskelf was built in 1770 and shows similarity with the mill on the Humber Bank, having common sails (mounted on a cast iron cross) and being winded by a Dutch-style tailpole. However, it seems to have been slightly shorter as there was no stage, the tailpole and sails being operated from ground level. The tower was constructed of stone halfway up and brick above, and for many years it has been cemented and whitened. The mill had three pairs of millstones.

The working life of the mill drew to a close by 1907 and some twenty years later it was bought by Mr Sam Sutcliffe of Bradford and converted to a dwelling. It did however retain a wind-power connection, as Mr Sutcliffe constructed a conical roof, embellished by an aeroplane propeller to generate electricity, but which only operated in a westerly wind. He obviously enjoyed living in the converted windmill as he is recorded as saying "You're never lonely living in a windmill. All your relatives come out to see you". A number of changes of occupancy have since occurred but the mill still presents an attractive and distinctive feature in this flat terrain.

Cawthorne
Clough Green Mill

NGR SE 272 075

A mill was noted in the 1770s to the west of the village of Cawthorne and half a mile south of Cannon Hall. As the land was outcropped for coal in the 1940s no surface features remain.

In 1809 John Claude Nattes, a topographical artist, was appointed as the drawing master for two of the five daughters of Walter Spencer Stanhope at Cannon Hall. Among much else that survives of his work is his drawing of this windmill. It shows many details of interest, including the domed cap and the tailpole supported by a cartwheel. Some of the red bricks of the tower were said to be re-used on the estate saw mill, near the present garden centre. As well as bricks, stone was used in the construction of the windmill, as can be seen around the base of the tower.

Beverley Westwood, Hither Mill
NGR TA 023 392

The long-standing post mill on this site was severely damaged by a storm in 1714. It was soon rebuilt only to suffer an identical fate in 1773. Being aware of the new tower mills being built in nearby Hull, the miller, Samuel Fenby asked his

landlords, the local Borough Council, for a new lease to enable him to replace the destroyed post mill with a brick tower mill, which he estimated would cost £200. The new lease was to be for 60 years at a rent of £6 per annum. The lease was granted, but the final building cost increased to £600 as a result of which the Council extended the period of the lease to 80 years. The mill had common sails and a tailpole but in this case, as the tower was no more than 35ft (10.5m) to the base of the cap, the sails and tailpole could be set from ground level and therefore a stage was not necessary. Hither Mill was subsequently modernised, so when advertised for sale in 1839 it was described as having five patent sails and a fantail. The mill was demolished in 1856 following the expiration of the lease.

Queensbury, Shelf Mill
NGR SE 125 292

Windmills have always been rare in the western reaches of Yorkshire, and therefore the survival into the twentieth century of the old tower mill, still at work by wind, in Burned Road on Shelf Moor was especially noteworthy. Said to have been built in 1789 and operated by members of the Barraclough family from 1852, the mill was a monument to early technology. It continued to work by windpower until 1904, with its domed cap and handsome finial, common sails and tailpole. The tailpole had a cartwheel at its base and a winch with a chain which could be attached to one of a series of wooden posts surrounding the tower, used to pull the cap round. This eased the task of the miller when turning the sails into wind.

The photograph of the mill being demolished in 1963 shows the massive size of the tower with its four storeys and basement. There was evidence to show that the brakewheel was originally turned by a wooden windshaft, later replaced by iron. The wood upright shaft was in four sections bound together. There used to be three pairs of millstones, the largest two of which were 5ft 4ins (1.62m) and 5ft (1.5m) in diameter respectively. Tentering, the means of adjusting the gap between the millstones, was by way of a lighter staff for one or more of the stones. This operated with a system of levers on a fulcrum, instead of the usual governors. It was another indication of the influence of Dutch millwrights, the lighter staff system being common in the Netherlands.

Stakesby

NGR NZ 892 108

The tower mill proved popular and once adopted by the corn millers spread fairly rapidly. Coatham had a tower mill as early as 1774 and three others appeared along the North Sea coast, where they were well placed for business. They were amid a wheat growing area and close to the sea which offered easy export opportunities. One of these mills was at Stakesby, built in 1778. It had common sails and an unusual cap (for Yorkshire) which shows some individuality on the part of the millwright. The cap was turned into wind using a winding wheel. At a later stage the mill at Stakesby was modified by the addition of patent sails and a fantail, in which form it continued to operate until 1877. It has now been demolished.

Etton

NGR SE 981 428

Until the standard design for tower mills became settled, one or two early attempts by local millwrights produced some interesting structures. Etton Mill was built around 1790 to replace a post mill at another site in the village. The tower is reached by a step ladder to a doorway at first floor level, reminiscent of access to a post mill. There is a separate door into the ground floor, and on entering it can be seen that the first floor is supported by an upright post which is quite clearly taken from a post mill. Was this mill built by a millwright who was more familiar with earlier practice and who wanted to make sure the stone floor was properly supported? If that was the case, when it came to the mechanics of the mill, he was more up to date with the technology. The sails were a combination of two spring sails and two roller sails and the cap and sails were turned by a rather individually designed winding wheel. The tower and the upright post still survive.

An anecdote told by descendants of the last miller gives an interesting insight into the life of a working miller. The windmiller is ruled by the weather, and thus if the wind gets up in the middle of the night, so does the miller. The miller's long-suffering wife became somewhat fed up with the disruption this caused to the household so she consigned the miller to a separate bedroom and had a ladder fixed beneath the window for his use on such occasions.

Pontefract, St Thomas's Mill

NGR SE 466 234

St Thomas's Mill stood at the top of Mill Lane at the corner of Orchard Head Lane from the earliest years of the nineteenth century. It was probably slightly larger than Etton Mill, having four pairs of millstones (compared with only two at Etton) and all four sails were roller reefing. The photograph, taken in the 1920s, shows its stone construction with patchy mortar added. It was rebuilt as a house with a prominent chimney and additional rooms. Estate housing encroached by 1963 and the tower was demolished before 1969.

It was sometimes called *Nevison's Mill* as a remembrance of the infamous highwayman of this area. Luke Ward was miller here from 1893 to 1908, having previously been at nearby Dandy Mill from 1877 to 1889. A delightful reminiscence heard by the redoubtable H E S Simmons was that this mill was always regarded as "... a good winded mill", doubtless in part due to its fine site, and would often be seen working when others in the neighbourhood were forced to remain idle.

Bramham
NGR SE 432 433

Bramham Mill, insured in 1794 but perhaps built earlier, is a good example of a small group of windmills in West Yorkshire where the mill appears to be built on a mound but in fact the mound covers what is in effect the basement of the tower. At Bramham the access to the mill was a doorway of ordinary width but in the other examples the doorway was up to 8ft (2.4m) wide, which would enable a cart to be driven into the basement for loading and unloading. The mound around the basement would have two functions, first to give access to the sails and tailpole, and secondly, to keep livestock away from the sails. The empty shell of the tower survives.

Aberford, Hicklam Mill

NGR SE 435 360

A similar mill to Bramham, and of about the same date, Hicklam Mill still remains in Aberford to the south of the village. It has a mound with a basement and three storeys above. There were originally two doorways at the level of the mound. This is an example of an arrangement which provides easy access to adjust sails and (probably) tailpole by hand, and a basement to increase storage capacity.

In 1817 the Wesleyan lay evangelist Sammy Hick from nearby Micklefield acquired renown when his prayer to God for sufficient wind to grind two loads of wheat for lovefeast bread was dramatically answered. A map published in 1849 shows this as *Old Mill* and in recent years there has been an attempt to convert the now derelict property into a dwelling.

South Kirkby
NGR SE 444 104

By the Old Mill Hotel in Mill Lane, South Kirkby, there was a variant of the previous two mills, which dated from the early nineteenth century or before. All round the stone tower was a covered area, built out as a gallery, all in stone, the height of the stone floor, supported by stone arches. Wide archways led into the tower. An ogee cap and at least two roller reefing sails were fitted. With the advent of a steam mill in nearby South Elmsall it became redundant and ceased work soon after 1880. It was used as a mission hall in 1915 but eventually left to decay, so that by 1972 all had gone except for a millstone in the grounds of Stockingate County Primary School where the mill stood.

146 N° 27.   OLD MILL, SOUTH KIRKBY.

Batley, Brownhill Mill

NGR SE 234 263

During the second half of the eighteenth century a group of tower mills, substantial in girth but with a rather squat appearance, was built. The majority were of stone and all were conical in shape. This gaunt, isolated tower stands in the playing fields of St Saviour's Junior School and Brownhill Infants School, about a mile from the centre of Batley. Most remarkably a contract survives for the reconstruction of the mill with new machinery in 1782. Two pairs of millstones, one grey and the other the more valuable blue, were installed, together with a new windshaft and brakewheel and a new upright shaft and spurwheel. The cost of the new machinery was £195. Later the mill was converted into a dwelling when the sloping roof was constructed, though this use of the tower ceased long ago. In 1999 the roofing slabs were removed for safety's sake, but fortunately complete demolition was averted. The mill still retains that heavy solid appearance, even though the slice was taken off when it was converted into a house. The mill was 28ft 6ins (8.6m) to the curb (so probably at least 40ft (12.2m) to the top of the cap) and the outside diameter of the base was 25ft (7.6m).

Askham Bryan

NGR SE 556 476

Though a mill is shown on this site on a road map scroll of John Ogilby dated 1675, unlike its partner at Askham Richard, the mill in Askham Bryan was a later replacement. Probably dating from the late eighteenth century, as with other mills of this period in more country locations, the tower had a very squat and bulky appearance. As such it later became a convenient advertising hoarding for the nearby Windmill Inn. In 1896 Elizabeth, widow of John Gilson, was both licensee of the inn and miller at the mill. She fell into debt about 1896 and the mill most likely ceased to work at about this time. By 1961 only low walls remained and now all is gone.

Leeds, Buslingthorpe Mill
NGR SE 302 356

A Leeds Landmark to Be Demolished

Two windmills on the north side of Leeds were once called *The Twin Towers of Buslingthorpe*. The tower of the more northerly, on Potternewton Mount, still remains while its partner, three quarters of a mile south and just north of Buslingthorpe Lane, has gone.

Insurance policies of the late eighteenth century show that both in their turn were owned by William Barrow, who also owned the Scott Hall watermill. By the middle of the nineteenth century a map called both *Old Mill,* and both had been converted into dwellings. Reflecting on his years in the mill, Mr Arthur Chadwick, in a newspaper report of 1938, looked forward, with the mill's imminent demise, to moving away but not without emotion. He said he used to enjoy sunbathing on the roof, but there were other days when the "wind whistles round the circular wall and the whole place seems to sing a song". He added "It'll be a change to have electric light - we've only had oil lamps here - and have straight walls to put wallpaper on ... It's only a year or two that we've had a water supply, and even then we've no hot water." In spite of all this, however, he was very proud that generations of his family had lived there right to the end of the mill's life.

Thurcroft, Carr Mill
NGR SK 515 899

The remnants of a bulky eighteenth century tower of magnesian limestone survived between Thurcroft and Maltby, until it was demolished in 1976. Only the outline of the base remains.

Morley, Gildersome Mill

NGR SE 249 288

The mill at Gildersome dates back to at least 1783 when it was insured by John Turton, the owner of nearby Turton Hall. The brick structure, with a similar cap to one of the Rotherham mills, looks as though it had patent sails fitted later, with a modern fantail added as well. This photograph of about 1885-95 shows the miller, Ephraim Ellis, who probably leased the mill, with his two children and, with particularly distinctive headgear, four 'masters' from Turton Hall Academy. Ephraim died in 1918 but the mill had already fallen derelict by the time of the photograph. By 1971 the tower had been demolished and the brickwork left where it fell. Opencast coal mining eventually obliterated the site, though an old narrow footpath, Stoney Pit Lane, still flanks the field boundary.

Leeds, Middleton Mill

NGR SE 314 297

Belle Isle and Middleton have seen enormous developments in the past fifty years or so, quite destroying the rustic air of Windmill Farm with its derelict tower, standing on rising ground behind the houses on the corner of Windmill Road and Middleton Road. This substantial tower had the characteristics of an eighteenth century mill. and had ceased to work by the second half of the nineteenth century. Now only street names, and the *Windmill Stores* nearby, keep the memories.

Leeds, Colton Mill

NGR SE 376 330

In 2006/2007 dramatic changes took place both in the neighbourhood of Colton Mill as well as within the mill precinct itself. Much new building, after years of gentle dereliction, included the renewal of the mill's tower with new windows and floors. The granary next to the tower and another building adjacent were both entirely rebuilt, but to a similar size as the originals.

A steam engine with a Lancashire boiler installed in the latter building was in use until about 1915. A gas engine which was "discarded two years previously at the Rothwell Picture House when talkie apparatus was installed" was used from 1931. The engine, with its flywheel 10ft (3.1m) in diameter, has now been restored but not to working order. The stone and brick tower remains inconspicuous but *Colton Mill* has happily become the name of the retail, hotel and office development all around.

Fishlake, Millfield Mill

NGR SE 648 140

A brick tower mill of three storeys was built in Fishlake in East Field Road about 1770. It had three pairs of millstones. In 1889 a horizontal steam engine was installed, signalling the end of windpower soon after. An older post mill in Wind Mill Road, a quarter of a mile further from the centre of Fishlake, was dismantled and its woodwork auctioned in 1839. This might have been used for a later post mill at Hay Green. The mill tower together with adjoining buildings have now been refurbished for use as a dwelling.

Stutton with Hazlewood

NGR SE 476 421

In recent years the stocky tower of Stutton Mill has become a dominant landmark for travellers on the Tadcaster bypass, but in earlier days it found itself in the middle of a large stone quarry. The tower of four storeys is finely constructed in magnesian limestone. The windows are unusually wide. A hearth has a flue through the tower to emerge next to a third storey window. Roller reefing sails drove two pairs of stones. Work ceased here and at the village watermill about 1890, both having the same owner at that date.

Sitlington, Sandy Lane Mill

NGR SE 277 175

The rough stonework of the tower of Sandy Lane Mill served to emphasise its diminutive size. An adjacent brick extension made this mill suitable for conversion to a dwelling and an auction notice of 1877 shows that it had become a home by that date. Its date of construction is unknown. At one time it served as a reserve for Cock Hill watermill at Horbury Bridge.

Mappleton

NGR TA 224 437

Above: The squat stockily built windmill was not limited to the stone mills in West Yorkshire, since several brick built examples could be found further east. Mappleton Mill was built in 1798 to replace an earlier post mill. Being located close to the coast it had all the wind it needed at this low height. Indeed, if built any higher it might have fallen foul of the strong East Coast winds. The mill continued in operation until the beginning of the twentieth century, after which it became one of the earlier windmills in the county to be converted into a dwelling and, refurbished, it remains in such use.

Speeton

NGR TA 147 748

Right: The village, a few miles north of Bridlington, is located at the top of Speeton Cliffs, some 135 feet above sea level. The tower mill, which replaced an earlier post mill, was very similar in design to the mill at Mappleton and was probably built around the same date. Unlike Mappleton it was fitted with four roller sails. It continued into use until 1901 and was eventually demolished in 1921.

Ugthorpe

NGR NZ 791 115

Left: A small squat tower mill was built at the end of the eighteenth century, probably on the site of a post mill. An early photograph shows the three storey tower with a ridged cap, winding wheel and roller reefing sails, with flat boards on the leading edge. At a later date, a fantail was added and John Harrison comments that according to some sources it had a cast iron mortise brake wheel and cast iron stone nuts. An advertisement of 1860 states that the mill had two pairs of millstones, one French, the other grey, together with a cylinder and all other conveniences "for carrying on to the greatest advantage the Business of a prosperous Agricultural Mill." By 1928 a third pair of millstones had been added. The mill has been converted into a dwelling.

Wentworth Windmills

NGR SK 392 982 & 379 987

Wentworth Woodhouse, the enormous eighteenth century mansion, presides over the countryside near Rotherham. Nearby Wentworth still has two houses which have been converted from windmills. The older, built in 1745 of dark red bricks on a stone base, is in Clayfields Lane. With the addition of battlements it was for a time called *Saxon Tower*. In 1793 it was replaced as a working mill by its partner at Barrow, half a mile away. In 1831/1832 a steam engine was constructed in Wentworth by the Milton Ironworks Company of Hoyland and the second windmill became redundant in 1834. Its fittings were sold at this point and the list of items for sale includes four roller reefing sails and an oak upright shaft, which shows the mill built in 1793 to have been "state of the art". But the list also contains interesting information of the state of milling at the end of the eighteenth century in that the mill was fitted with five pairs of millstones, two pairs of which, one of blue and one of grey, were still *in situ*. It is likely the other three pairs of millstones would have also been blue stones, as the preference for white flour was developing rapidly at this time. Blue or cullin stones (and later French stones) were used to produce white flour, as it was easier to dress the bran out of the meal produced with this type of millstone.

Rotherham Windmills

NGR SK 431 929 & 431 930

Right: Where the College of Arts and Technology has been built in the centre of Rotherham, between Eastwood Lane and Doncaster Gate, there once existed two windmills. They both dated from before 1774 but were very different in appearance. The smaller had a single storey outbuilding around its circumference, two pairs of millstones, four sails and a pyramid cap. The larger had three pairs of millstones and, by 1838, had been fitted with five sails. The town needed two mills in early days but following the introduction of steam milling in Rotherham by 1822 they had become obsolescent. An old decorative stone in the Rotherham Museum came from a barn standing "next to the windmills which were a landmark for miles around".

Seaton Ross, Preston's Mill

NGR SE 774 417

Left: The development of the eighteenth century tower mill owed much to the experience gained from Dutch millwrighting practice, but the basic structure, in the hands of the British engineers and millwrights, was improved significantly. Cast iron replaced timber shafts and gear wheels and practical experiments by the Yorkshireman, John Smeaton, confirmed the most efficient sail plan. Others invented the fantail, the spring sail, the roller sail and eventually the combination of these two, the Cubitt patent sail. All these new devices introduced an element of automation and self-regulation which greatly improved the task of the miller.

Preston's Mill was built somewhere between 1795 and 1810, to replace a long standing post mill. The photograph illustrates well the mechanism of the roller sail, patented by Captain Hooper in 1789 and which became fairly widespread in Yorkshire, no doubt due to the fact that the local millwrights, Norman and Smithson, became licensees for the patent.

The rolled up canvases are clearly visible in the sail frames, together with the V linkage to the striking rod, and the wheel at the back of the cap carrying the looped chain which the miller used to open and close the canvas rolls. It can also be noted that the sails were fitted with boards along the leading edge, which worked as air brakes. The outer end of each board could be rotated through ninety degrees to break up the air flow across each sail and thus reduce the speed. At the time of the photograph, the moveable boards had disappeared on four of the sails, but can be clearly seen on the fifth. The empty tower survives.

Knottingley
Wentcliff Mill

NGR SE 479 237

Here was another tower mill of magnesian limestone with some added brickwork, and likely to be of early nineteenth century date. There were four floors but no basement. A walkway with a maximum height of 3ft (0.9m) partly surrounded the tower. There was probably also a domed cap and finial. The mill used to be called *Nickey's Mill*, perhaps in remembrance of William Nicholson, the tenant miller of Fryston Manor for twenty years from 1837. Working by wind ceased in 1909 and the tower was demolished about 1967.

Mr and Mrs Barker, the last occupants of the farmhouse that stood by Wentcliff Mill, overlooking Ferrybridge, remarked that it was "... in a very isolated, rural spot with only a few cottages nearby". Now Mill View is but one of the many roads amongst the houses which cover the area.

Hull, Holderness Road Mills

Up to the 18th century the mills which served the residents of Hull were post mills located to the west of the town outside the Beverley Gate. During the eighteenth century the town began to spread westwards, as a result of which the old post mills disappeared. Replacement milling capacity was provided along Holderness Road, which ran eastwards from the town, the land on either side having been recently re-allocated under an Enclosure Act. The replacement corn mills all took advantage of the Dutch technology but were built by local millwrights who made considerable improvements to them, particularly using cast iron for much of the shafting and gears.

The detail from an engraving of 1865 shows some of these new windmills along Holderness Road. Mill D was the first to be built, in 1775, and had five common sails, the number recommended by John Smeaton, following his experiments. The next to be built was Mill F, in 1786. The millwright was probably James Norman, who a few years later was to join with Robert Smithson, to take up the licence to use Hooper's Roller Sails. When built the mill had five common sails, but in 1793 the new firm fitted six roller sails. Although five sails were the most efficient, corn millers were concerned that if one of the five sails was damaged, the mill would be out of action until a new sail was fitted. If, however, the mill had an even number of sails, when one was damaged, the counter-balancing sail could be removed and the mill continue in use (albeit with reduced power) until a new sail was available. It is probably with this in mind that when Mill E was built in 1794, only four sails were provided.

The other mills in the print are: Southcoates Lane Mill built in 1819 (A), Hull Anti Mill (B), Blockhouse Mill, built in 1806 but by 1865 converted to oil milling and powered by steam (C).

At the date this print was produced there were some 26 windmills in Hull. The only survivor is Eyre's Mill q.v.

Newport

NGR SE 854 304

The various mills built in Hull around the turn of the century clearly influenced the design of new windmills in the area, as the quality of the workmanship was commented upon by more than one person. For example, in 1811, Abraham Rees in his Encyclopedia, described them as "... the largest and finest in the Kingdom of this kind ... their machinery is excellent and many are from eighty to upwards of a hundred feet in height".

Sir George Head later wrote (in 1835):

"On leaving Hull, the number of windmills that meet the eye together give a character to the flat range of country which constitutes the district; standing still in one spot, within a mile of the town, I counted no less than 25 all of brick, beautiful structures, unusually high and circular. This type of building is now so perfectly understood and the bricks so well made and assorted, that not the least detriment is experienced from the stress and jar of the machinery; in short, they are models of windmills each with an ornamental cap or dome of wood, cast iron windshaft and fantail."

One of the windmills which met the eye would have been Newport Mill. When built, in 1797, it had either common or roller sails and, to facilitate access to the sails, a wide braced stage was provided. The patent sail became common in Yorkshire after about 1810 and when they were eventually fitted to Newport Mill the stage was reduced in width. The corbels on which the supporting struts rested can still be seen in the photograph. The mill was demolished in 1913.

Chapel Haddlesey

NGR SE 575 265

A cherry tree set in a garden at Chapel Haddlesey is on the site of a tower mill. The mill was built of stone with brick dressings. This indistinct photograph shows four double-shuttered sails (probably patents) and a tall ogee cap and fantail. A map of the 1770s provides evidence of a rather early date for the mill, and in 1829 it was for sale with three pairs of millstones, French, blue and grey. The sails blew off about 1896 and the tower was demolished in 1927.

Beverley Westwood, Jakeman's Mill

NGR TA 027 386

At the beginning of the nineteenth century the town of Beverley had one watermill, one post mill, one private tower mill and the newly erected Subscription Mill, but this did not deter speculators from erecting further mills. One such was a mill built for George Jakeman, on land adjacent to the Westwood, only a couple of hundred yards from the new Subscription Mill. It would appear Jakeman was under-capitalised from the start as the mill had to be sold to pay off his debts, which included part of the cost of building the mill. As a result of the sale we have documentation to show that the mill was built by Norman and Smithson and, like most mills built by this company, it had five roller sails. The new owner was more successful and the mill continued in operation until 1893. The lower part of the tower survives, incorporated into a dwelling.

Millers were in a privileged position. Being the providers of flour for making a most vital food, customers had little choice but to buy their products. This inevitably caused resentment, and pilfering from mills seems to have been a common occurrence. In 1849, the press reported that "... we understand that the gang of robbers who at present infest the neighbourhood, made another attempt to rob Mr Lowson [the then tenant] of Westwood Mill, but we are glad to say were unsuccessful in gaining admittance". The report then goes on triumphantly, "Some of the bacon stolen from Mr Lowson about one month ago, has been found in Hull, and it is hoped these midnight burglars will ere long be found out and punished".

Beverley Westwood, Black Mill

NGR TA 021 390

Another venture on the Westwood Common was the mill now known as Black Mill. When originally built, in 1803, the mill was fitted with four common sails and a tailpole, access to which was gained by way of a wide, braced stage. Once the new patent shuttered sails were fitted such a wide stage was not necessary and it was reduced in width. The photograph (which pre-dates 1868) shows the mill with patent sails and a narrow stage. However, the corbels around the tower which held the struts needed to support the original wider stage can still be seen. The empty mill survives today as a prominent landmark, although the corbels have disappeared.

Anti, Subscription and Union Mills

PREMISES OF THE
HULL ANTI-MILL INDUSTRIAL SOCIETY (LIMITED)
FOUNDED, 1795—REGISTERED, 1862

Lithographed by Jas Archibald from a Photograph by W J Wallated

Hull Anti-Mill
NGR TA 113 298

During the last decade of the 18th century the corn market was still subject to the prohibition against the importation of cheap wheat and millers were frequently blamed for the high prices. Bread which had cost a *penny farthing* per pound in 1768 had advanced to *tuppence hapenny* per pound. Consequently in 1795 certain poor inhabitants of Hull *to preserve themselves from the invasions of covetous and merciless men* formed the Hull Anti-Mill Society. These Hull co-operators proposed to pay 1s1d per week for four weeks and thereafter 5d per week for four weeks more, towards building a flour mill which the subscribers and their heirs might possess for ever. Having reached this point they petitioned the mayor and corporation for further assistance. With help from individual members of the council the mill was built on Holderness Road and opened for business in 1797. In true co-operative style the opening ceremony included a procession, led by a band, followed by an elegant dinner at which two crown bowls of punch were drunk. The original membership was 1,435 and the mill cost upwards of £2,200.

The illustration on the right (dated 1800) shows the structure as it was when first built - a very tall tower, claimed by the local press to be the largest windmill in England. It was fitted with five roller sails, an early form of fantail, and a braced stage to provide access to the sails and striking gear, etc. During its life the mill was adapted and improved, first by the conversion to patent shuttered sails and a fully developed upright fantail, and later by the addition of steam power. The illustration on the left shows the mill as it stood at the end of its working life in 1895. There is no documentary evidence to identify the builder but there must be a strong presumption that it was the work of Norman and Smithson. The mill was demolished in the 1930s.

Beverley Union Mill

NGR TA 022 385

The idea of forming a co-operative quickly appealed to the residents of Beverley. A meeting of the "... poor inhabitants" was held in 1799 to discuss the "... great inconvenience experienced and in future likely to be experienced by the high price of flour". The Society was formed; they raised the necessary funds, and the Town Council, who were highly pleased with the idea, agreed to make a piece of ground on the Westwood Common available. They also contributed 56 guineas towards the scheme. Councillor Tuke added 10 guineas of his own money and the Society gratefully placed their account with his bank, Messrs Harland and Tuke. The foundation stone was laid with due pomp and ceremony on 31st July 1800.

The mill was very similar to the other subscription mills, except that it was perhaps not as tall. The truncated tower remains today, incorporated into the Beverley and East Riding Golf Club clubhouse.

Whitby Union Mill

NGR NZ 894 111

The concept of co-operative milling spread further afield. In Whitby a similar society was formed in 1800 "... to relieve the suffering of the poor ... considering the very high price of wheat and the frequent practice of grinding inferior grain (so) that

good bread is difficult to procure. It was noted that the people of Hull have found much relief by such institution". The foundation stone was laid on the 16th June 1800, beating the Beverley project by some five weeks.

The mill was some eight storeys high with five roller sails when built and was very similar to the contemporary Subscription Mill built in Hull. It is more than likely that the mill was built by the same millwright who built the Hull mill. The Society was clearly influenced by the Hull Society; what better than to use the same millwright? It would be a simple matter to transport the materials and parts by sea from Hull Docks to Whitby. The mill was demolished in 1909.

Hull Subscription Mill

NGR TA 107 296

The Hull Anti-Mill Society was highly successful, so much so that a second co-operative, the Hull Subscription Mill Society, was formed. On the 12th July 1800 the foundation stone was laid in Dansom Lane and the mill opened for business on the 1st July 1801.

This mill was another colossal structure, some nine or ten storeys high and with five roller sails. Again there is no documentary evidence as to who built this mill, but the design is virtually identical to the successful Anti-Mill and there can be little doubt that it was built by the same millwright. The mill was demolished around the time of the Great War.

BOREAS Union Mill 181º

Pontefract, Boreas Union Mill (Dandy Mill)

NGR SE 468 230

Intriguing puzzles remain concerning the history of this mill. Over the first floor window facing Water Lane is the inscription, in beautifully executed lettering, giving its name -

BOREAS Union Mill 1819

Boreas is the north wind, a fine title for a windmill. But why is the first word in one style and *Union Mill* in another? The inscription is also over a former doorway, which surely must have been intended as the principal entrance to the mill, except that it happens to be one floor up. The brickwork of the present ground floor, with one narrow doorway, is splayed out, so that perhaps it might have been intended to have a basement, if soil levels at that time permitted. The mill eventually became known as *Dandy Mill*, by which it is still affectionately known today.

The mill had three pairs of millstones on the third floor, rather than the more usual first or second floor. Its proximity to the railway embankment, built in 1845, would have caused turbulence, especially with a north wind blowing hard! One tradition is that the owner lost money here and built the mill at Darrington instead, but in fact the mill continued in use by wind power until 1922 and thereafter was powered by a gas engine until 1941.

Kilham Union Mill
NGR TA 060 641

Kilham Mill was a brick tower of five floors, probably about fifty feet to the curb and is photographed with four patent shuttered sails, a fantail of individual style and a narrow but braced stage. This cannot have been its appearance when built in 1809, for it would have had common or roller sails, which would have necessitated a wider stage. Once the patent sails were fitted the stage could be reduced in width, as happened elsewhere, but here the bracing was retained. Another decidedly odd feature is the location of an external pulley at fourth floor level. There are a number of cases where windmills had an external pulley fitted, but they were usually at low level and connected to the spur wheel by an upright shaft. This arrangement enabled the mill to be driven by a steam engine. However, it would have been rather difficult to connect a (portable) steam engine standing at ground level to a pulley some thirty or forty feet in the air, with an on-going problem of trying to prevent the belt from falling off!

In addition to some of the questions regarding the mechanics of the mill, there is also a puzzle as to its ownership. An advertisement of the 1st July 1809 offers for sale the *Union Mill at Kilham*, in which it is described as "newly erected and (in every respect) extremely convenient and well built". The advertisement goes on to say that it "was constructed under the direction and superintendance of an able and experienced Millwright". Unfortunately there is no clue as to the name of the *able and experienced millwright.*

However, the mill sold very quickly, the formal documents conveying the property to the purchaser being signed on the 21st and 22nd of August. The documentation shows that there were five trustees "of the wind corn mill lately erected by subscription at Kilham", five members of "the committee for the time being appointed to superintend and direct the concerns of the mill" and a largish number of subscribers. The purchaser was William Hutchinson, a tanner from Hunmanby who had recently resigned from that business. By 1823 the miller is shown in the directories as John Williams until sometime between 1858 and 1872, when Robert Chandler took over. He remained in possession until 1913. The last miller is recorded in 1933. It appears therefore that the mill was financed by subscription but as soon as it was built, it was sold to a private owner. It has not been possible to ascertain why this happened but there could be several reasons. The committee may have been unable to find and appoint a suitable miller, or it may be the committee and the trustees could not agree amongst themselves (as happened elswhere). The tower has been converted to a dwelling.

WINDMILLS IN THE NINETEENTH CENTURY

Patrington Haven Mill

NGR TA 309 219

By the end of the first decade of the nineteenth century a standard form of tower mill had emerged. The form is exemplified by Patrington Haven Mill, built in 1810 by a new firm of Hull millwrights, G & W Boyd. It was built of brick, had five floors, and a rather squat ogee cap and four patent sails. There was also a fantail, which by this date had developed from the rather simple horizontal device seen in the early illustration of Hull Anti-Mill, to the elegant framework which held the fan higher and thus in better air flow. By the end of the first decade of the nineteenth century, the combination of the patent sail and the fantail made the working life of the miller substantially more comfortable.

It has been noted earlier that the basic layout of a small tower mill comprised three floors:
> (1) the grain cleaner and storage bins on the higher floor,
> (2) the millstones on the middle floor, and
> (3) the floor delivery chutes and bagging up systems on the lower floor.

The addition of two or more floors would give the miller more storage space and the opportunity to install extra plant, in particular a dressing machine to extract the bran from the meal to produce plain flour.

The original owner was a Mr Nicholson who seems to have let the property rather than operate the mill himself. Interestingly his tenant in 1879 was Henry Sanderson, who appears to have carried out a millwrighting business as well as running the mill, as in 1888 he auctioned off a whole range of millwrights tools. The mill was offered for sale shortly after that and acquired by a Mr Connell, in whose family it still remained when milling by wind ceased in 1928. The empty tower is now used as a store.

Seaton Ross, Fisher's Mill

NGR SE 777 421

This is another example of the standard windmill, a five floor brick tower mill built between 1814 and 1823. The later tower mills have less batter to the walls of the tower than the earlier examples. Also the entrance is some 3 or 4 feet (1 to 1.3m) above ground level, with a little platform to facilitate unloading a cart. The empty tower is today used as a store.

Bainton

NGR SE 963 527

Built in 1817 Bainton Mill was a typical East Yorkshire tower mill. A press advertisement of 1819 indicates that the mill had three pairs of millstones, two French and one grey. This became the most common arrangement for the village tower mill, producing white flour for the daily bread and animal feed, particularly for the horses, which were still the major power source for farm work and road transport. Note the miller sitting on the sail frame! The empty tower survives.

Hutton Cranswick

NGR TA 022 531

The mill was in existence by 1816. In that year the miller, Thomas Chambers, was declared bankrupt. The documentation describes him as a farmer and miller, and it is quite clear that many of the millers who operated village mills had sufficient spare time (and need for spare cash) to combine two businesses. The mill was dismantled in the 1870s but the tower survives, also in use as a store.

Beeford

NGR TA 131 535

Described as *newly built* in 1820, Beeford Mill had four patent sails and a fantail. When built it had only two pairs of millstones but by 1880 a third pair had been added, together with a barley mill (for polishing pearl barley), a screen for cleaning the wheat prior to grinding and a dressing machine to extract the bran. The original miller, George Whiting, died in 1820 and the purchaser, James Booth, became bankrupt ten years later. Nevertheless, in spite of this inauspicious start, the mill continued in business until 1933. The truncated tower survives in use as a store.

Apart from the problems of finance and the hard work involved in running a mill, millers sometimes succumbed to less technical problems. Shortly before Christmas 1868, a body was found drowned in a ditch at Beeford. It was discovered that the unlucky man worked for a nearby miller, but the inquest did not seem very sympathetic, simply noting that he had been out with his cart that day delivering orders and as was the custom at the season of the year, it was supposed he had imbibed several glasses of ale or spirits on the road.

Sproatley

NGR TA 195 345

Built in 1820, Sproatley was another example of the standard East Yorkshire tower mill. It comprised a brick tower of five floors, the walls of which were modestly battered. The mill was fitted with three pairs of millstones, two French and one grey, showing that it was designed to serve both the local farming community (i.e. producing both flour and animal feed) and the comparatively close-by residential area of Hull Town.

Perhaps understandably, this well-built mill attracted the interest of one John Rank, the son of a miller who had been employed at several mills in Hull. Rank occupied Sproatley Mill in 1825 and when three years later he bought the mill, it became the very first of many mills to be owned by the Rank family. John remained until 1841 when he left to take possession of a mill in Hull. Milling continued until 1892 and the mill was demolished a few years later.

Gilberdyke, Scalby Mill

NGR SE 849 300

The story of this mill is both uncertain and unusual. The uncertainty arises from the fact that there were five windmills in the vicinity of Gilberdyke and the adjacent village of Newport and, in the various press advertisements, they are frequently given conflicting names. Scalby Mill is sometimes referred to as *Anti Mill* which indicates a co-operative venture similar to those seen in Hull, Beverley and Whitby. Unusually the mill was built by Sanderson's of Louth, a well known Lincolnshire millwright, and the design of the sails was slightly different from the norm in East Yorkshire. In this design the shuttered sails are attached to the wooden arm (the *back*) which is fixed to the cast iron cross on the windshaft. In the usual East Yorkshire pattern the leading edge is almost as wide as the driving side or trailing side, whereas Sanderson's leading edge is considerably narrower.

When the mill closed, around 1933, much of the milling gear was sold to Messrs Rose, Downs and Thompson, a Hull foundry who cast many parts for windmills and were famous for their oil seed presses. The mill was demolished between 1933 and 1943.

Hollym

NGR TA 353 249

Below: At the start of the nineteenth century, Hollym had a post mill which continued in operation until 1879, when it was dismantled and all the machinery laid out in lots on the site. By 1855 a second mill, the tower mill, had appeared which continued in operation until the 1920s.

The photograph shows the cast iron cross on which the sails were mounted and the timber beam immediately behind the cross which carried a bearing (the neck bearing) to support the outer end of the windshaft. The small platform in front of the door was used to unload sacks from a cart. The mill last worked by wind in 1921 and had been demolished by the start of World War Two.

Ellerby

NGR TA 170 389

Above: In 1830 the mill was described as newly built and was owned by the Hull millwrights G & W Boyd. It is likely therefore that the mill was either built by them as a speculation or, more likely, the person for whom it was built had been unable to pay the bill. The mill has been converted into a dwelling.

Muston

NGR TA 107 799

Above: Muston Mill was built about 1820/30 to replace an earlier post mill. It comprised a brick tower with four patent sails. A miller is last mentioned in 1913 and it probably went out of use shortly after that date.

Langtoft

NGR TA 005 680

Langtoft Mill is situated high in the Wolds on a site which had been occupied by a post mill since at least 1729 and probably a lot earlier. The post mill was replaced by the present tower mill sometime during the mid-nineteenth century and continued in operation into the 1920s. In the early 1980s the mill was converted into a dwelling.

Snaith, West Cowick Mill

NGR SE 649 218

Although this site at West Cowick appears to have been used for milling at least since the eighteenth century, the four storey red brick tower looks much more like a nineteenth century rebuilding, though a slight change in outline betrays some further alteration. The mill went out of use during the First World War and in 1928 was demolished, together with a granary building, leaving only the mill house prominently remaining in Mill Lane.

Monk Fryston
NGR SE 507 292

Right: Although originally built towards the end of the eighteenth century, the mill was substantially rebuilt after storm damage in 1818 and can properly be regarded as a nineteenth century mill. The ground floor was built of magnesian limestone but the three upper storeys were constructed of brick. By 1834 a steam mill was added, but eventually all the property was cleared away for housing in 1953.

Barwick-in-Elmet
NGR SE 395 370

This grand six storey tower mill with its finely proportioned ogee cap once stood on the western edge of Barwick-in-Elmet. It possessed four pairs of millstones, including one of the high quality blue stone. The tower was built at least by 1819, though steam power was in use here by 1851. Joseph, son of the miller Thomas Warrington, was killed by lightning at the mill in 1852. Mr Tommy Kirk, who worked here in the early years of the twentieth century as a carpenter, remembered the story that his grandfather was bet a gallon of ale if he would hold on to a turning sail and turn round with it, up and over. He won! With sails gone by 1912 and the supplementary engine only sporadically used to the 1930s, the ironwork later went for scrap and the tower was demolished in 1951.

Cantley
NGR SE 633 018

Cantley Mill in Green Lane is halfway between Cantley and Branton. The limestone foundations point to a mill here before the present brick tower with its weatherworn date stone of *W C 1820*. Three pairs of millstones on one floor were augmented by a fourth for the steam engine on a floor below. The nearby chimney for the engine has a date stone reading *W C 1845*. W C refers to William Carr who was the owner of the property at least from 1801 to 1862. The engine last worked in 1927 and the structure remains virtually empty. The Parish Council investigated the scope for preservation in 1978/1979 but nothing more has since been done.

Darrington
NGR SE 474 199

A red brick tower, once covered by tar, still stands boldly at the end of a range of rolling hills near Pontefract. It is one of the few in Yorkshire that retains some of its original machinery. The tower, built about 1820, stands to a height of nearly 46 ft (13.9m), consisting of a basement with five storeys, with a blind dust floor above. There was once a slope down to a level below the basement floor to permit easy loading and unloading when wagons were drawn up at the entrance. Windows in the basement indicate that there was no mound built up around the tower but access to the ground level is only to be found at one doorway, which incidentally is three steps up.

Three overdriven pairs of millstones remain with a train of gearing which connects to the spur wheel. There was once a machine for producing rolled oats. A fireplace with its flue is another feature of the tower.

In about 1903 the mill was tail-winded on a stormy Sunday night. A mill suffers this fate when the wind swings round rapidly to strike the sails from the back, causing the sails to try to turn in the opposite direction, or worse. In this instance the last miller, George Featherstone, lost his nerve in dealing with the situation; he let the sails turn and one sail was thrown. Windpower was not used afterwards. The Home Guard took over the mill during World War II when a secure roof was inserted at the top of the tower, and this in turn has helped to preserve the structure.

Appleton Roebuck
NGR SE 543 425

A long-established site of a windmill halfway along a track from Appleton Roebuck to Bolton Percy was last shown on a map of 1817-18. When a map was published ten years later it showed that a new mill had been built half a mile to the west of Appleton Roebuck, and the first was no longer marked. The red brick tower, once tarred, and with stone sills, used to possess three pairs of millstones, a wire dresser and gearing for an external engine. Work had ceased here by 1885 but the empty tower still remains.

Ackworth, High Ackworth Mill
NGR SE 442 178

For a time there were two windmills and one watermill working in Ackworth. The first windmill, built by the middle of the eighteenth century, was situated at the Moor Top end of Mill Lane, while the watermill was at the other end. Both windmills are shown on a map of 1823-24. The photograph shows the second windmill, which stood at the top of Mill Hill, not far from the centre of High Ackworth. A steam mill was later added here with its chimney standing close to Jubilee Terrace. Eventually all was replaced by a bungalow, called *Millston*, built about 1960 but a good reminder of earlier days.

Airmyn

NGR SE 725 258

When Frances Eglesias was staying as a guest of the Wells family at Boothferry House in 1873 he painted this picture of a view looking north to the Earl of Beverley's Clock Tower in Airmyn. The River Aire is on the left-hand side and Airmyn Windmill is shown about a quarter of a mile from the tower. The engraving is by Rock and Company of London and dated 1880. Rather strangely the painting looks as though it depicts a postmill and the engraving a tower mill. It is recorded in 1834 that the mill was "... substantially built and works three pairs of stones ..." This probably indicates a tower mill but the painting still looks convincing as a post mill! It was said to have gone before 1900.

Hatfield Woodhouse

NGR SE 671 087

Right: This mill, built in 1836, with a tower 50ft (15.2m) high and 20ft (6m) in diameter, means that here at Hatfield Woodhouse was a powerful symbol of the new breed of windmill. About one fifth of its height is of magnesian limestone and the remainder brick. Three pairs of millstones, and two more when steam power was added by 1872, indicated an industry of considerable importance beyond the immediate village setting. It was not to last, however, for by about 1900 windpower was no longer used here and steam ceased at much the same time. The tower, now decoratively embattled, together with the adjacent engine house and granary above, is now used merely as a store.

Conisbrough

NGR SK 520 985

Left: The empty tower of this fine mill at Conisbrough, built in coursed blocks of magnesian limestone, was demolished in the summer of 1979 and now houses cover the site. It stood to the south of Crookhill Road and about a half mile from the Castle. It was first noted in a letting notice of 1840, offering the mill with "... shade sails and three pair of stones, screen, dressing machine, &c." Work probably ceased here well before 1900.

Fishlake, West Nab Mill

NGR SE 652 131

Right: A standard type of tower mill remains at West Nab in Fishlake. A four storeyed red brick tower with three pairs of millstones, it was probably of mid-nineteenth century date, and a late addition to the milling capacity for the village. It became disused by 1893, and has been converted into a dwelling.

Swinefleet Tower Mill

NGR SE 780 228

Left: This is another standard mid-nineteenth century brick tower mill. H E S Simmons recorded two pairs of French millstones and one pair of peaks. Other detail included the information that its windshaft, brakewheel and upright shaft were all of wood, while the wallower and eight-spoked spur wheel were iron. It was tail winded in 1923 but milling continued afterwards with the aid of a tractor connected via a large pulley. All became disused in 1933 and the top storey was removed. Now, no longer derelict, the remaining tower has been transformed into a substantial dwelling.

Ousefleet

NGR SE 828 231

Right: Ousefleet Mill stood at the corner of Hall Garth and is another example of the standard mill. Of four storeys, with a fantail and patent sails, it was built about the middle of the nineteenth century and contained two pairs of stones and a dresser by W Pindar of York. It had a wooden windshaft but the upright shaft was wood through the top two storeys and iron below. The mill's working life ended when it was tailwinded before 1943 and it was demolished some time later.

Bishop Burton

NGR SE 993 393

Below: A fine example of the East Yorkshire windmill of the general design of mills built in the area after about 1810, but with a stage at third floor level. Stages were usual on the early tall tower mills, to give access to the tail pole and the sails, but here the stage had a different purpose. By the end of the eighteenth century, millers were no longer simply milling grain brought to the mill by their local customers. Now the millers were buying grain from farmers and selling their own products to bakers and grocers. This meant that more storage space was required than was available in the mill tower. Thus, as at Bishop Burton mill, additional buildings were erected, linked to the tower. The miller still had to gain access to the brake rope and the chain by which the patent sails were controlled, which could be at any position around the tower, dependent upon wind direction. So, to obviate the need for the miller to scramble over the roof of the linked buildings, the stage was added to provide a walkway round the tower. Note the doorway through which access on to the stage could be gained from inside the mill. Access was only required to the striking chain and brake rope, and not required for setting the sails or using a tailpole. Consequently the stage could be made much narrower than was the case with the earlier examples.

The truncated tower has been converted into a dwelling.

Patrington, Goodrick's Mill

NGR TA 320 223

There is some doubt as to the date Goodrick's Mill was built. It is recorded that the son of the last miller, James Goodrick, claimed in 1936 that the mill was built in 1845. However, prior to the present mill, there was a post mill on this site and an advertisement in the *Hull Advertiser,* dated 20th May 1809, offers for sale a "... good substantial post mill" which after sale must be "... immediately taken away from the premises". It seems likely the mill was built shortly after 1810. James Goodrick only acquired the premises in the 1890s. The tower is now used as a farm store.

Thearne
NGR TA 071 361

Built in 1815, Thearne Mill is a good example of the East Yorkshire windmill. A tall tower with stage, the batter of the tower wall being fairly minimal, winded by fantail and fitted originally with four roller sails, later converted to patent sails. The mill had three pairs of millstones, two French pairs and one grey. The premises also included a kiln, a feature found fairly often in the eighteenth century but less so in the nineteenth, used for drying grain, particularly barley. The mill was disused by 1926 but survived until final demolition in the 1950s.

Easington

NGR TA 397 199

Above: Built around 1815. It is reported in *The Miller* of November 1907 that the owner, Mr Charles Biglin "... has had the windmill ... refitted and brought up to date for flour making, with the result that the mill has taken a new lease of life, to the advantage of the district." Unfortunately the new life was curtailed when in March 1911 the sails "... suddenly broke off and crashed down". Fortunately no one was injured. The mill was finally demolished in the late 1920s.

Hornsea

NGR TA 197 479

Right: Built in 1820, Hornsea Mill is interesting, being the only mill we can be certain was built by Messr Todd and Campbell, iron founders of Hull. The firm certainly made iron castings for other millwrights and later, under the name of Rose, Downs and Thompson, became world leaders in the manufacture of oil crushing machinery. As one might expect, much of the machinery was made of cast iron. What is unexpected was the fact that the shutters in the patent sails were made of sheet iron. The mill has now been converted into a dwelling.

Aldbrough Tower Mill
NGR TA 237 386

Right: Built by 1823, this mill originally had a stage, the access door being clearly visible in the photograph. Windpower ceased to be used by the end of the nineteenth century, but the mill was not demolished until the late 1930s.

Swanland
NGR SE 988 278

Below: Swanland Mill is another example of the tall tower mill with a narrow stage. Note the tower is less conical as seems to be the pattern for later tall mills. The picture illustrates the sad end to this mill. In December 1893 the fantail was damaged in a storm. According to a local eye witness "... various sections of the fan were blown clean out, some flying great distances and being found three miles away". The miller attempted to carry on without the fantail, but then a tower mill is at the mercy of the weather, and the miller must attempt to turn the cap manually. This is an almost impossible task in a large tower mill and inevitably the mill soon became *tail-winded*, i.e. the wind blew from the opposite direction to the way the sails were facing and as a result the shutters were blown forward. Finally in March 1895 the main shaft broke in a severe snowstorm and the mill never worked again. When advertised for sale in September 1895, it was said ominously that "... it is an excellent and very eligible situation for the erection of villa residences, being within twenty minutes walk of the Ferriby Station." The mill was demolished in 1908.

Ryhill

NGR TA 222 268

This is an example of a tower mill with a stage added - note the window access to the stage. The photograph gives a very clear picture of the *gallows fantail* construction which was common in East Yorkshire. The mill appears to have been demolished before World War 1.

Pudsey Mills

NGR SE 222 321 and SE 214 328

The history of windmills in Pudsey seems to be controlled by the frequency of their damage or loss by fire. The Moravian Settlement at Fulneck was established in the 1740s and a windmill was a necessary adjunct to the community. In 1806 an existing mill was destroyed by fire and a new one in Mill Hill was built. It is pictured on the aquatint, of which the illustration is a detail, by Charles Henry Schwanfelder (1773 - 1837). The complete picture shows a view of Fulneck looking north from the valley and is dated 1814. Fire again caused damage in 1823 and it seems that steam milling for the Moravians, as well as for Pudsey inhabitants in general, took over at that time.

A later windmill was built in Windmill Hill in the Smalewell district of Pudsey but it appears to have survived for only a few years in the middle of the century. Its remains were demolished in 1927 leaving just a hole in the ground.

Norton

NGR SE 538 148

Prominently sited south-west of Norton village is the white tower of the windmill. Once it was derelict but from 1975 transformed into a very considerable dwelling, with refurbished tower, a new ogee cap, and substantial additions. The site has been occupied by a mill at least since 1750 but the present structure is certainly later. With five storeys of stone it used to have a gallery at first floor level. Its working life continued to at least the beginning of the twentieth century.

Sheffield, Attercliffe Mill

NGR SK 383 895

Attercliffe has seen many changes through the years and it seems a far distant time when this imposing giant of a windmill was to be seen in the area. First coming to notice in 1811, the mill was part of the property of Don Bank House which had "... beautiful grounds with a fine front garden sloping down to the wooded riverside". The six storey tower of tarred brick possessed a stage at second floor level, a fine ogee cap, a high fantail and four roller reefing sails. Four pairs of millstones were accommodated. Later a steam engine was installed, the chimney of which bore the date *1832*. Houses gradually encroached on the area in the 1860s and the mill eventually ceased work in 1881, succumbing to demolition a couple of years later.

Goole, Timm's Mill

NGR SE 740 239

Two mills were built in Goole during the time that the town was being developed in the 1820s. One of these was the five-sailed mill in Boothferry Road. It was both higher and wider than its contemporary, later called Heron's Mill (see p.104), though both originally contained three pairs of millstones. By 1854 three pairs of French stones, now with a steam engine, had been added in a building next to the tower. It indicates an increasing emphasis on the production of flour compared to animal feed.

Edward Timm purchased the property in 1868 and through the years he and his family continued to improve and enlarge the capacity of the enterprise. Windpower was eventually abandoned in 1892, and the old tower was later extended upwards for a water tank. The business continued to prosper until 2001 when closure regrettably came. Plans were made for the use of the site for retail shops and housing, but for the moment the gaunt tower alone survives on the site, hopefully ready for a new phase of its life in the future.

Skelton

NGR SE 375 696

Magnificently sited on the skyline from the Great North Road, Skelton mill in its heyday must have presented a fine sight for miles around. Dated 1822, with six storeys of stone, a stage at second floor level, a tall ogee cap, four sets of millstones and almost wholly cast iron shafts and gears, the mill began its life with five sails, but these were later reduced to four sails. The earlier photograph is of about 1885 and the second ten or more years later. In spite of its modernity the mill ceased work about 1918, and then slumbered into dereliction. In 1962 work to make it useable began, though complete conversion to a dwelling was only completed in 1996.

Thorne, Gravil's Mill

NGR SE 686 137

The last of Thorne's mills to survive stands on the northern side of North Eastern Road, the route along which six of the town's seven mills stood long ago. This may have replaced one built in the eighteenth century. When for sale in 1827 it had new patent sails and four pairs of millstones with dressing and screening machines. Steam power was introduced in 1832 when a further three pairs of millstones were added. A very prominent loading platform used to be evident, further indicating the substantial business here through the years. The end of wind power came in 1904, but a 12hp compound portable engine by John Fowler of Leeds enabled trading to continue for further years.

Whitby, Newholm Mill

NGR NZ 862 096

However one tries to classify windmills, there is always an exception. The mill at Newholm was "... totally destroyed by fire ... nothing but bare wall left standing" in 1822. The mill was certainly rebuilt and by 1831 it was in the care of miller John Appleton. Thus the mill shown in the photograph, by F M Sutcliffe, must show the mill as rebuilt soon after 1822. The photograph shows a six storey, stone-built tower with ogee cap, fantail and four roller reefing sails. There were certainly a number of mills which retained their roller sails, long after the patent sail became standard, but to find what was in effect a new mill built some twenty years later being fitted with roller sails is unusual. The mill had a narrow stage but with the bracing normally associated with the wider stage one finds on earlier mills. A miller is last mentioned in 1913 and the mill was probably demolished shortly after that date.

Hinderwell

NGR NZ 792 166

Built in 1828, Hinderwell Mill was an elegant stone tower mill, some seven storeys high. An advertisement in the *York Gazette* of May 1830 claims ".. the machinery was executed by a first class workman without regard for expense". In 1868 a meeting was held at a nearby inn, "... it having been considered by many persons desirable to convert the [mill] into a union mill in £5 shares". It is not clear why this should have been considered at this date, but the project seems to have failed and the mill carried on in private hands. Steam power was added in 1872 but the mill ceased to function before 1900. All the machinery was removed in 1915, but the date of demolition is not recorded.

High Hawsker
NGR NZ 925 076

High Hawsker Mill, built around 1860 by George Burnett, was severely damaged by fire only a few years later, in 1868. Nevertheless it was repaired and carried on working into the 1920s. The truncated tower survives, in use as a farm store.

Ingleby Barwick, Sober Hall Mill
NGR NZ 447 129

Sober Hall Mill is part of an interesting group of buildings, comprising a granary (the long building at the rear), a horse wheel shed (the rectangular building in the centre) and the windmill. The granary is thought to predate the two mills, the dates of which are uncertain, but it is likely the windmill was built in the 1820s. The tower is said to have stood at its full seven storeys in 1914 but by 1930 had been reduced to four storeys, and survives in this form.

Redcar

NGR NZ 609 250

Sober Hall Mill was one of over a dozen tall tower mills on the southern side of the Tees. Three of these were situated in Redcar, just south of the point where the river discharges into the North Sea.

The mill to the left of the picture was Redcar Mill, a large six-sailed mill built between 1801 and 1833. To the right of centre can be seen the remains of Coatham (Marsh House) Mill which was in existence by 1774 but severely damaged by fire in 1815. For some reason it was not rebuilt but a new mill, shown to the right of the picture, was built in its place. This tall mill, with four sails and fantail, ceased milling at the time of World War I, when the tower was used as an observatory. It was finally demolished in 1934.

Sherburn - in - Elmet

NGR SE 493 337

The tower mill in the centre of Sherburn-in-Elmet, close to the present Royal British Legion Club, was built about 1860 as a replacement of a mill a half mile further south. An unusual twelve-bladed fan and a flattish ogee cap topped an imposing five storeys of brick. Under the lowest floor was a brick waterproof cellar into which rainwater was piped, a useful feature in dry summers for a village with no mains water at that time.

At the turn of the century John Charles Rhodes combined his work as miller with work as a solicitor, while twenty years later Mr Habesh was not only the miller but also the proprietor of the adjacent cinema.

In 1921 fire enveloped the mill when it was in full working order. Without a good supply of water a fire engine from Selby was unable to cope and the mill was destroyed with an insurance loss of nearly £5000.

Hatfield, Lings Mill

NGR SE 660 083

The substantial remains of earthworks are not normally associated with windmills, but at Hatfield, at the junction of Doncaster Road and Lings Lane, a two level mound survives, in the form of a circle on a square, known to be the site of an early post mill which existed until the 1850s. Another post mill stood a quarter of a mile away in Lings Lane until it was replaced in 1878 by the present red brick tower mill. This was one of the last windmills to be constructed in Yorkshire and dates from the same time as the virtually identical Wrancarr Mill at Moss.

Steam power was introduced by 1888 but only twenty years later was replaced by a paraffin engine. The sails were blown off in 1912 and all milling ceased here in the 1920s. Ezra Williamson, who helped build the Lings tower when he was fifteen years old, and who subsequently worked at Lings Mill, spent his later working life at a new steam mill in Manor Road until his death in 1937. The steam mill was later changed to operation by gas and continued in operation until 1973. The empty tower of Lings windmill survives.

HATFIELD.

Sale of a Post Wind Corn Mill.

MR. R. J. COULMAN

WILL SELL BY AUCTION,

ON THE MILL HILL OF THE
HATFIELD LINGS,

On Thursday, Nov. 25, 1875,

ALL THAT POST WIND

CORN MILL

With two pairs of French Stones, Machinery, Gearing, Scales, Weights, and Fittings as she now stands, being situate on the Hatfield Lings, Hatfield, the Property of G. Hatfield, Esq. The sails are good and complete.

The Mill with her Materials and Appurtenances to be cleared off the Ground on or before the first day of January, 1876.

SALE AT 2 O'CLOCK, PROMPT.

No Reserve, and for Cash.

Auctioneer's Office, Thorne, Nov. 9th, 1875.

Hartley and Son Printers by Steam Power, Chronicle Office, Doncaster.

Moss, Wrancarr Mill

NGR SE 594 128

Wrancarr Mill, or as it is sometimes known, Trumfleet Mill, just south of the settlement of Moss, is said to have been built about 1880 and is of identical measurements to Lings Mill at Hatfield, built in 1878. A post mill on the other side of the trackway to the tower existed at least until the early years of the nineteenth century.

The tower has four storeys and was equipped with two pairs of millstones. The fine photograph is by Paddison of Doncaster, noted photographers between 1900 and the first World War. Mr Duckett, who used to dress the stones, is on the left-hand side of the photograph. Wind power ceased to be used here in 1917 due to damage by lightning, though by then the curb gearing in the cap was well worn too. A Blackstone oil engine was later installed, connecting with the gearing in the tower but, in spite of this, all milling still ceased by about 1928. Ironwork except for the cast iron halves of the cap finial went for scrap during World War II. The shell of the building remains secure.

Sykehouse

NGR SE 625 174

It was in the beautiful summer of 1867 when an old post mill at Sykehouse was removed and a new tower mill built on the same site. The sum of one hundred guineas due to the Snaith millwrights for their work was counted out in sovereigns by Elizabeth Mary Wigglesworth, a young visitor to the owner, George Ward Sail. His cousin, George William Bullas, took over the running of the mill in 1904 and in due course married Elizabeth Mary. Their son George continued the business when George William died in 1917. Sykehouse Mill had five storeys and a blind half-storey at the top. The final four working sails, of double-shuttered patent variety, were put up by Wilson's of Thorne. Three pairs of millstones were installed, and an oat roller and bolter for grading flour increased choice for their customers. In 1917 an additional pair of stones was installed, operated by a Hornsby oil engine from the adjacent engine house. In total this made two pairs of peak and two French. In latter years it was William Stainton who did the day-by-day work of milling.

A family photograph, taken just before the turn of the century, shows proud parents, Elizabeth Mary (née Wigglesworth) and George William Bullas. Their children are (left to right) in the back row, Ada, William, Annie and Mary; in the middle row are Emily, Robert in the arms of Elizabeth, Laura in the arms of George William, and Amy, and in the front row George (who succeeded as miller), Clara and Kitty. It was the youngest son Robert, born in 1898, who in 1980 remembered his work in the mill both as a boy and in later years.

William Hutton used his dray to collect grain from farmers within about a four mile radius, in the districts of Balne, Pollington, Snaith and Cowick, and afterwards to return it processed as required. The dray had its sides painted with the inscription -

G W BULLASS / MILLER / SYKEHOUSE / SNAITH / YORKSHIRE

George's brother, Robert, remembered that production of flour ceased in 1919 and provender only was milled afterward. The end came altogether in October 1935 when the sails were blown off in a gale. Sykehouse Mill has therefore the dubious honour of being the last mill to work by wind in the West Riding.

The tower was converted into a dwelling in 1972, at which date the oil engine was rescued and is now preserved at Worsbrough Mill Museum in the watermill cared for by Barnsley Metropolitan Borough.

Goole, Goolefields Mill

NGR SE 758 213

Thomas Birks was the owner of Broadbent's Mill in Goole until he was obliged to leave, being faced with the impending development of the town. His name, or that of relatives, appears here from 1867 onwards. The present red brick tower has a bold inscribed stone *T.B./1871*, the date of a late replacement of an earlier mill. Work ceased here about 1890, so that the tower was only in use about twenty years. The empty tower was offered for sale in 2007.

Bridlington, Duke's Mill

NGR TA 180 688

Right: Later in the nineteenth century, in some of the more exposed villages, there was a return to the smaller tower. One example was Duke's Mill, built before 1823, a small free-standing tower mill, the internal diameter of the base being only 18ft 6ins (5.6m), and fitted with four roller sails and winded by fantail. The mill only had two pairs of millstones, both French, and it must have been a highly speculative venture, as there were already six established windmills and three watermills in the town by this date. The final remains of the tower survived until the 1990s.

Wilberfoss

NGR SE 724 514

Left: The village of Wilberfoss had been served by a post mill which unfortunately was destroyed during a gale in 1838. The owner, Mr Rowntree, decided to replace it with a brick tower mill. The brickwork was erected by Thomas Gray, the village bricklayer, and although the mill is said to have contained some very old timbers (no doubt salvaged from the post mill), much of the shafting and gears were made of iron.

In 1946 a three year old nephew of Mr Rowntree, John Bell, came to live at the mill. Later he became tenant and remained at the mill until he died in 1938, just short of the mill's 100th anniversary. The mill was demolished around 1970.

Leven New Mill
NGR TA 117 453

Right: The village of Leven was connected to the River Hull by a straight three mile long canal, which put the village in an advantageous position. Three windmills were located near to the canal head, one by coincidence being a long-established post mill. It is recounted that the miller fell out with his neighbour, who retaliated by planting trees along his boundary which interfered with the steady flow of wind to the mill. Consequently in 1847 the post mill was abandoned and a new mill built at the eastern end of the village.

This was very similar in scale to the mill at Wilberfoss, being only four storeys, but with all the usual East Yorkshire features. The mill has been demolished.

Garton
NGR TA 261 358

Left: This charming little mill stands in a field which still contains remains of the ridge and furrows of the medieval farming system. Built in the late 1830s, the windmill stands some 35ft (10.6m) to the curb and still contains a significant amount of its original equipment. The construction seems to be a one-off, most of the shafting being of timber, which suggests the mill was built by a local carpenter or wheelwright.

Heslington
NGR SE 628 509

Right: The miller at Heslington also had trouble with trees on neighbouring property but when this occurred, sometime in the 1920s, the miller was an old man and decided the better course of action was to retire. The mill remained idle for many years gradually deteriorating, although complete with all its plant and equipment, until 1941 when it was demolished by Messrs Robson of Walmgate, York. The ironwork went for scrap and the brickwork from the tower was used as hard-core at Rufforth Aerodrome.

Old Malton

NGR SE 793 740

A modest three-storey brick tower mill, which probably dates from the second or third decade of the nineteenth century. It lost its sails in 1906 and may have gone out of business at that date. The tower is now used as part of a dwelling.

Ravenscar
NGR NZ 976 006

It is suggested that the mill at Ravenscar, opened in 1859, was a speculative venture but too late to be profitable. The proprietor, William Hammond, an auctioneer from Middlesex, had recently bought the Raven Hill estate and it is thought he was expecting the nearby alum industry to expand, resulting in more people coming to live in the locality. But by this date the chemical industry had started to produce synthetic mordents and the production of alum from the local shales was rapidly declining. The mill did serve one useful purpose for Hammond, when in 1858 part of the wedding reception for his daughter was held in the unfinished mill!

The material for the rusticated stone tower came from the sandstone overlying the alum shales and the tower still stands, empty and unused.

TOWER WINDMILLS RAISED IN HEIGHT

Bempton

NGR TA 189 713

Although this mill is shown on the early OS maps as Bempton Mill, it is actually just over the border in the adjacent parish of Sewerby. Built originally as a small three storey tower mill, the structure has at some stage been raised in height. The mill was most probably originally fitted with common sails which would be accessible to the miller from ground level. However, the mill was subsequently converted to patent sails, which could be adjusted by way of the striking chain hanging at the rear. There would be advantages in raising the height of the tower. The sails would turn above head height of anyone standing at the side of the tower, thus removing the risk of injury and also the miller would have extra storage space available. Furthermore, the extra height would raise the sails higher into the wind, although this might not have been so important here as the mill was at a high point not far from the cliff top. The land around the mill is now used as a caravan site, with the mill tower being used as an office.

Skidby

NGR TA 020 333

Built in 1821 to replace an earlier post mill, Skidby Mill was originally a four storey mill, with sails reaching down or near to ground level. However, when the lease became available in 1854, it was taken up by Joseph Green Thompson, thus establishing a family connection with the mill which lasted until the mill closed down in the 1960s. Joseph was a progressive miller and in order to expand his business he needed more space. To achieve this he added a range of buildings, either side of the tower, which in turn necessitated it being raised. These buildings also had additional plant installed at various dates and it was a simple matter to take a drive shaft from the tower into these new buildings.

The original builders were the leading firm of Norman & Smithson, and their work was of a high standard. However, the alterations to the internal layout, carried out by the Howden millwright, George Reed, when the tower was raised, have an air of *making do* about them. The alterations involved in particular raising the millstones from the first to the second floor. It was also necessary to add a stage, access to which was via a window on the new stonefloor. The mill is now owned by the local authority which has converted the premises into a rural museum.

Yapham

NGR SE 790 505

Built in 1805 by William Daniel, millwright of Pocklington, who probably had an involvement with the several watermills in this part of the county. Yapham Mill has also been raised in height, in this case either to allow for, or because of, buildings erected around the tower. The millstones were left in their original position, although it appears likely a third pair of millstones was added. The tower and much of the equipment survives (but not in situ) and it is apparent the work is of a high quality.

York, Holgate Mill

NGR SE 584 515

Left: The precise history of Holgate Mill is still the subject of research, but it seems likely that it was built around 1770. At this date it would have been fitted with five common sails, the arrangement being recommended by John Smeaton as the most efficient. The method of winding the mill is not clear; tailpole or winding wheel were known in the area at that date, but Smeaton has shown that the horizontal tailpole was in use in Leeds about this date, so such may have been used here. At some date (probably by the end of the 18th century) the common sails were replaced by five roller reefing sails and, later still, the five roller sails were converted to patent sails. When the roller sails were added the tower was raised in height, to enable the sails to turn above head height of anyone standing at the side of the tower and thus removing the risk of injury.

Holgate Mill is undergoing a complete restoration to working order.

Hunmanby

NGR TA 095 763

Right: Another example of a mill raised in height was that at Hunmanby, built in the late eighteenth century and obviously raised when patent sails were added, the increase in height being just sufficient to enable the sails to turn above the top of the doorway. Hunmanby has had its own mill for several centuries and a document, dated 1732, sets out certain local laws made by the Lord of the Manor down the years. Four of these relate to the miller and give an interesting indication of how the miller fitted into feudal society. The jurors of the Court Leet were obliged to visit the mill after a court session and "... grind or cause to be ground" all sorts of corn and "... observe diligently" what the mill yields after the toll had been deducted. Toll was the share of the flour which the miller was entitled to take in payment for grinding it. If a juror failed to carry out this duty he was fined 6/5d. If the miller took more than the allowed toll, he was fined 10/-. The owner or occupier of a mill was also required to keep a "... sufficient" miller there. For every month without, he was fined 10/-. Additionally, the miller had to grind wheat brought to the mill in the correct priority, starting with the owner of the manor, then a freeholder in the manor, then a tenant or inhabitant of the manor and lastly, anyone from outside the manor. For each default he was to be fined 3/4d. The mill went out of use in the 1920s but the derelict tower remained until after WWII.

WINDMILLS ADDED TO WATERMILLS

Cottingham

NGR TA 048 334

At the start of the nineteenth century there was still a number of watermills operating in the Hull Valley, albeit with varying degrees of success. One such was at Cottingham, an area rapidly developing as the preferred residential area for the businessmen of Hull. The unreliable nature of the water supply to the long-standing watermill made it impossible for the miller to meet the demand and his only option was to add wind power to his premises, which he did in 1813. This proved successful and his example was followed at other watermills along the Hull Valley, namely Beverley Parks (1822), Foston-on-the-Wolds (1822) and Bryan Mills, Lockington (1840). The mill was demolished in 1900.

Ellerker
NGR SE 923 298

Although not in the Hull Valley, Ellerker Watermill was located at a point on the southern limit of the Wolds and the miller decided to follow the example of Cottingham and the other mills, by adding a windmill in 1822. The photograph shows the windmill in course of demolition, giving an opportunity to see the gearing inside the cap. The cast iron cross which held the four patent sails can be seen, and gives an indication of how the sails were fixed to the cross. Each arm of the cross had a single bolt which passed through the iron of the cross and the timber of the sail - the king bolt. The sail was then held further by either three or four *bridle irons*. The cross was mounted on the cast iron shaft, which is set at an angle. This allowed the sails to turn without hitting the brickwork of the tower and transferred some of the weight of the sails and windshaft on to the rear (tail) bearing. The brakewheel, made of timber but with cast iron cog segments, can be seen between the two men standing to the left. Protruding from the front of the cross can be seen the outer end of the striking rod. The striking lever, from which one end of the striking chain is hung, is evident too. Also visible are the two massive timbers which pass fore and aft (the cap sheers).

Goodmanham

NGR SE 885 425

Goodmanham Mill was sited about one mile to the east of Market Weighton, in a short valley which cut into the scarp face of the Wolds. In earlier times the valley had been crossed at this point by the Roman road which ran northwards to York, from the crossing of the Humber at Brough. In later years this valley provided the route for the railway running eastwards from York via Market Weighton to Beverley.

A small stream running down the valley provided power for the first mill on this site, a water powered paper mill, built probably around 1800/05. Several paper mills appeared in the area about this time but this particular venture appeared to be unsuccessful, probably as a result of the competition and the inadequacy of the water supply. The water was taken from the stream via a leat which ran along an embankment to a mill pond but the stream relied upon springs rising a mile or so up the valley and, as was found elsewhere, springs were notoriously unreliable. Consequently between 1813 and 1818 the mill was converted to a corn mill and to deal with the unreliability of the water supply, a windmill was added. The poster advertising the sale in that year claimed that "The Mill has patent sails, Dressing Mill, etc. and is in every respect quite complete, and capable of doing much business...". A miller is last mentioned in 1913, by which time the mill was probably driven by an auxiliary engine.

The photograph shows the premises as they stood around 1900. The building on the left was the mill house, the windmill was incorporated into the centre of the range and the building to the right was the watermill. The mill pond was behind the watermill and the tail race ran under the forecourt to discharge back into the stream to the right of the picture. The mill buildings were eventually demolished in 1940 at which date the millhouse and outbuildings were incorporated into an attractive dwelling.

A SMOCK MILL

Goole, Broadbent's Mill
NGR SE 748 232

Goole has a unique place in the history of Yorkshire windmills. When the Aire and Calder Navigation was first cut it followed the route of the Aire to West Haddlesey and from there struck northwards by a cut-off canal to Selby. Eventually the proprietors became dissatisfied with this situation and they wanted a more direct route to the Humber and the sea. Goole, originally just a small village on the banks of the River Ouse, became the destination for the through route from Knottingley.

The project meant that from about 1822 the proprietors began to purchase land and property for docks. They also had the intention to build a small but flourishing town. One purchase was a house owned by Thomas Birks, together with his windmill on the banks of the Ouse. This is where Broadbent's windmill becomes unique amongst Yorkshire corn mills, for it was not the usual brick or stone tower mill, but the wooden version known as a smock mill. Such mills are common in parts of south east England, and more especially Holland and Northern Europe. No doubt easy access to supplies of timber on this riverside site helped the decision to build a cheaper style of mill here, but there could also be influence from over the seas.

The mill must have been demolished soon after its purchase. It was simply in the way of new devlopment.

THE ADDITION OF STEAM POWER TO WINDMILLS

Keyingham Old Mill

NGR TA 244 256

The drawing (dating from about 1900) of the old mill at Keyingham illustrates many features of the typical East Yorkshire windmill, the four patent sails, the gallows fantail, an extended tower, and the general layout of the equipment, but of particular interest at this point is the steam engine, a semi-portable engine rated at 14hp. It is ironic that at the very moment in time the English windmill achieved a level of construction second to none, the steam engine, which had rather stagnated in the late eighteenth century, started to develop. The critical development was the use of high pressure steam, thus paving the way for the production of smaller and less expensive engines.

The steam engine was installed at Keyingham sometime before 1891 and the diagram shows how this was achieved. An upright shaft took the drive from the sails down to a large gear wheel (the spur wheel) immediately above the millstones. This is a standard way of conveying the power to the millstones and other equipment in windmills. The steam engine is connected by belt to a pulley on the outside of the tower which, via a pair of bevel gears, is connected to a second upright shaft. This takes the drive from the steam engine up to the spur wheel although this drawing has a touch of artistic licence in that it would be impractical to leave the sails connected to the spur wheel whilst the mill was being driven by the steam engine.

Internally, Keyingham Mill is the most complete example of an East Yorkshire windmill and is still cared for by members of the Eyres family, who have owned the mill since the mid 1880s.

Lelley

NGR TA 219 326

Left: Steam power was added to Lelley Mill somewhere around 1860. The engine was located in the building to the left of the picture and was probably a larger engine than that at Keyingham. The boiler still survives on site but not *in situ*, and a very fine chimney stands next to the mill tower. The belt drive was protected from the weather by the timber-clad structure which passed diagonally up to the tower, at a point just below the stage. As was often the case when steam power was installed, at Lelley two additional pairs of millstones and two extra dressing machines were installed. The tower with most of its machinery, including the boiler from the steam engine, survive but in a very derelict condition.

Sutton

NGR TA 114 333

Right: Sutton Mill exemplifies several stages in the development of Yorkshire windmills. When built around 1777, it replaced an earlier post mill. At that date it comprised a modest free-standing tower with a steeply battered wall, probably no more than three storeys high.

At some date the tower was raised in height quite dramatically to some seven floors, with a high stage at second floor level. Five patent sails were fitted, using a cast iron cross, though the leading edge of each sail was extremely narrow by East Yorkshire standards. Having reached this state it was an impressive structure and, being set in fairly flat ground, was visible for many miles around.

By 1876 a double-cylinder, vertical high-pressure steam engine, with a 9ins cylinder and 20ins stroke, had been added by Messrs Fowler & McCullin. The flywheel was 12ft (3.6m) in diameter and steam was supplied by a Cornish boiler, 22ft (6.7m) long by 5ft 6ins in diameter. Rated at 20hp, the engine enabled ten pairs of millstones to be added, together with a number of dressing and cleaning machines.

In many cases where a basic mill was extended from time to time, and a large amount of new plant installed, extensive shafting was required to connect the new and old equipment to the new and old power sources. Such shafting involved a considerable number of bearing blocks, each of which required regular greasing to prevent the block from running hot. Alas, in April 1884 a column of smoke was seen rising from the mill as the premises were burnt to the ground.

Dalton Brook
NGR SK 454 943

This photograph taken in the 1930s of Dalton Brook Mill, north east of Rotherham, shows the remnants of a rather elongated tower at least six storeys in height. It was mostly built of stone, though some untidy brickwork additions have also been made. An ogee cap and an iron cross to which the sail frames were fixed are shown. This mill also had a steam engine with a very fine chimney but the date when wind power ended here is not known. Nothing now remains of the site.

Walkington
NGR TA 001 378

The evidence is not clear but it seems Walkington mill was built fairly late, possibly about 1850. However, it is reasonably clear that the steam engine was added in the 1880s. The mill was demolished in 1971.

Kippax Mill

NGR SE 426 299

Kippax Mill is possibly a unique example of a windmill erected but converted to steam power before the sails were added. The first map to show Kippax Mill is dated 1827. Remarkably, by then not only the tower is shown but also the engine house and chimney on one side and the granary on the other. A beam engine was recorded here with a 12ft (3.6m) flywheel.

The material for the tower, the granary and the lower half of the engine house, is stone, with the rest brick. It looks as though a decision to use steam power rather then wind power was made as soon as the tower was constructed.

Some neighbouring towers have a basement and a mound to give access to the sails and striking mechanism. Here there is a basement but no sign of a mound. A ladder is used to reach the floor where the top of the mound would otherwise have been. Roughly cut inside-doorways as afterthoughts link the three spaces. Work stopped here about 1917 but a Hornsby gas engine was noted in the 1940s. Today, oats are ground in the tower, albeit with electricity and modern machinery.

WINDMILLS USED TO PUMP WATER

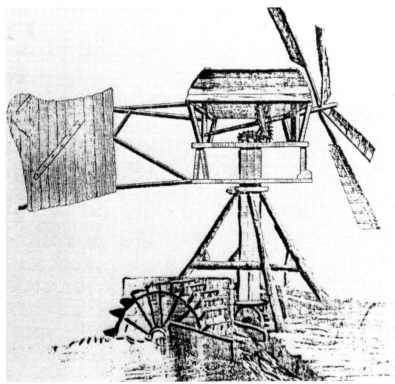

Routh

NGR probably TA 105 416

There are a number of situations where water needs to be raised, either for drainage or into a storage tank for a specific use. In many cases the power requirement is comparatively small but must operate reasonably continuously and with a minimum of supervision. In Yorkshire, small wind-powered pumps have provided the answer since at least the seventeenth century. An example of such a mill is known to have existed at Routh near Beverley, where it was used to drain water from agricultural land into a nearby ditch. It was a simple hollow-post mill, driving a small paddle wheel, in effect a water wheel working in reverse. In 1764 a scheme which proposed to use five of these little mills was prepared by John Grundy in conjunction with John Smeaton to improve the drainage of land to the east of the River Hull. However, although drainage works were carried out, there is some doubt as to whether these mills were ever built.

Hull Brickworks

The extraction of clay for brick making soon produced a number of large holes in the landscape and when the next shower of rain descended, the impervious clay would hold the rain water. The resultant pond would be extremely inconvenient to the workers seeking to extract further clay. To overcome this problem, brickyards in the county made extensive use of the wind-powered bucket pump, which appeared in two forms. One, as used at Hull, was a simple hollow-post mill, with a skeletal buck holding the cranked windshaft which drove the bucket pump at ground level. There were several brickworks in and around Hull and it is not known in which of these this particular pump was located.

Catfoss Brickworks

NGR TA 137 460

Right: Another example of a skeletal hollow-post mill which drove a bucket pump was set up at Catfoss. It was built before 1900 and was still in existence in 1935.

Broomfleet Brickworks

NGR (Broomfleet) SE 865 270 etc.

Left: A number of clay pits were dug at Broomfleet, which required no fewer than six of the wind-powered bucket pumps. One at least was a hollow-post type, similar to that at Hull. We have on record an account from a Mr Kitching, the last operator of this mill. He explains: "I have had several struggles with this pump - it was my responsibility for several years and this pump being the most powerful it took much more strength and know-how to stop and reef down ... During gale force winds you had to get several men to hang on the chain and pull the mill around sideways to the wind direction, dash up the ladder on to the platform, slap the friction brake on, grab the nearest sail and make it captive by the hook and chain on the frame ...

At ground level where the top of the pump barrel and spout are situated was a barrel which contained upwards of 50 gallons of water. This was used for priming the pump after you had got her in motion. You were always pleased if you got the pump primed with 10 or 15 buckets of water - needless to say the first thing you did when you got her pumping was to refill the barrel and say here's to the next time."

The available photographs of the hollow-post mill version, show the buck as skeletal, i.e. without any weather board cladding. However, one of the post mills is reputed to have been rescued from Broomfleet, after which it was first re-erected in a private garden. By 1997 it had been transfered to the Yorkshire Museum of Farming at Murton Park near York. At that stage the buck was clad with weather boarding but, although it was clear some alterations had been made to the structure, there is no record as to whether it was ever clad in this way when *in situ*. Unfortunately the structure has disappeared from the museum and its present whereabouts are unknown.

Elvington Brickworks

NGR SE 683 470

Left: The second, and more permanent, form of these brickyard pumps comprised a slim brick tower, usually between 20 to 25ft (6 to 7.6m) high. The frame which held the windshaft was mounted on a cast iron curb around the top of the brick tower. In a large corn mill the cap frame was maintained in position by its own weight, plus a number of centring wheels which prevented the frame from sliding off the curb. In the case of these windpumps, the weight of the frame was not sufficient. Consequently the framework which held the windshaft was mounted on an iron ring, which fitted between two matching rings attached to the top of the brick tower. These two rings were set sufficiently apart to allow the windshaft framework to rotate freely. The mechanics of the machine were otherwise the same as the hollow-post mill version. The wind pump has been restored to working order by the owner.

Howden Brickworks

NGR SE 752 311

Below and below left: These small mills were usually fitted with common sails but in some cases, as here at Howden, they were fitted with spring sails. The wind pump has been restored to working order by the Howden Civic Society.

Claxton Brickworks

NGR (Claxton) SE 692 596

The slender towers of these mills made access to the windshaft for maintenance purposes somewhat difficult, in particular for regular greasing. So at Claxton an external ladder was attached to the windshaft framework to ease the operator's task. The structure is now well *protected* by ivy, as a result of which the iron and timber machinery is still practically complete, although the timber has suffered considerably more than the ironwork.

There were a large number of brickyards in the county. Further examples of the use of these wind-powered bucket pumps are known at Doncaster, Hewarth Moor near York, three examples at Selby (East Common Lane, Bondgate and Mount Pleasant), Newport, Kexby, Breighton, Hemingbrough and Sandholme, but there must have been many more.

At Bank Top near Brighouse, a stone quarry also used a wind-powered pump but details of its construction have not been ascertained.

Acaster Malbis - Naburn Drainage Mill

NGR SE 596 457

Above: An example of the tower mill type, called Naburn Mill though actually on the opposite bank of the River Ouse in Acaster Malbis, was maintained by the local Drainage Board in its working days. Mr G Atkinson, the ferryman at Naburn, was in charge of it, with his father before him. In the spring of 1940 the sails, by then dilapidated, blew off and it was intended to replace the tower with a metal windpump. In the event, however, the tower was kept, and a Climax windvane pump installed on the top of the old tower. Now all has gone.

Eastrington, Bloomhill Farm

NGR SE 808 331

Below: Flood protection banks have been constructed alongside many rivers in East Yorkshire which, in some cases, required a wind pump to lift water from adjacent fields into the river. The pumps used were similar to those used in the brickworks, and one stood in the fields of Bloomhill Farm adjacent to the River Foulness. In this case, only the cranked windshaft survives, so we cannot be sure which of the two types of wind pump was erected here.

Hornsea Railway Station

NGR TA 208 477

Below: The pumping mills mentioned previously were all intended to remove water from places where it was not required. However, there are a number of examples where wind power was used to provide water for specific purposes. One such example occurred at Hornsea Station, where a rather unusual windmill was built around 1864 by the Hull and Holderness Railway Company to lift water into a header tank from where it was fed by gravity to locomotives. It remained in use until the end of steam on the line but the final remains were not demolished until the 1980s.

Goole Cemetery

NGR SE 762 243

Above left: North of Goole on the road to Hook is the site of the town cemetery; its chapels are dated 1877. The cemetery, adjacent to the River Ouse, used to be waterlogged and some form of drainage became necessary. The answer was to use a wind-powered bucket pump of the type in use at the brickworks.

In this case, no doubt to respect the dignity of the location, the frame holding the windshaft was covered with an ogee cap, a miniature version of the caps on the large corn windmills, but which were not considered necessary on the pumps in the brickyards. The structure lasted until 1930.

91

WINDMILLS USED FOR INDUSTRIAL PURPOSES

Hull, Moore's Oil Mill
NGR TA 098 302

Grinding various types of corn into flour was a simple process but seeds which had a higher oil content required a different process. Rape and line (flax) seed were particularly valued for their oil content, which was extracted by first crushing the seed and then, after warming it to make the oil run more freely, pressing it to squeeze out the oil. The device used to crush these seeds comprised a circular flat bed on which a millstone mounted on its edge, was rolled around. In earlier times, the stone was moved by a horse but by the mid seventeenth century, wind-powered oil mills had started to appear.

One such was in Hull. It is recorded that in 1719 Joseph Pease had purchased and repaired an existing tower mill standing in Church Street, which drove oil crushing machinery. In 1747 he replaced this mill with a much larger one, built by a Dutch millwright, which was probably the forerunner of the very tall tower mills built in Yorkshire. It is also recorded that, within a few years, John Smeaton replaced the poll end of the timber windshaft with a cast iron cross.

There are no illustrations of the Pease Mill but in 1781, Joseph Moore & Son built a wind-powered oil mill nearby. The picture of the mill as it stood around 1894 shows it to have been identical to the details we have of the mill built by Joseph Pease. The mill was demolished early in the 20th century.

Hull, Salthouse Lane Oil Mill
NGR TA 100 289

Left: Joseph Pease originally had three oil mills in Hull, one in Church Street, as already described, one a horse mill and the third, a windmill in Salthouse Lane. This mill is unusual for England as it has all the appearance of a Dutch wip mill (hollow-post mill) in which the buck is simply a rather large gear box with the drive being taken down to machinery at ground floor level. This mill was built by 1735 and demolished in 1800 when Pease decided to concentrate his activities at the mill in Church Street.

Hull, Maister's Oil Mill
NGR TA 102 292

The Maister family had an oil mill in Wincolmlee which was driven by a post mill, probably a hollow-post mill similar to the one operated by Pease in Salthouse Lane. Around 1810 it was decided to replace the post mill with this much more substantial tower mill. The combined influence of the Dutch practice and Smeaton's sail layout, both very influential in Hull during the last quarter of the eighteenth century, are well illustrated in this picture. The mill was destroyed by fire in 1866.

Wakefield Oil Mill (Westgate)
NGR SE 332 208

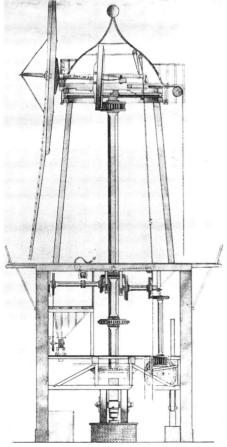

John Smeaton (1724-92), the celebrated engineer of one of the Eddystone lighthouses, of much canal development and other public contracts, designed three windmills in Yorkshire. In 1754-55, after studying Dutch practice, he built the windmill in Wakefield. It was on the south side of Westgate at its highest point.

The windmill had a two storey square base 28ft (8.5m) in height. This housed all the machinery including the edge runner stones for pressing rape seed for oil. The owner, Stephen Roodhouse, was prohibited from using his mill for grinding corn in order to protect the owner of the monopoly, or soke, Sir Lionel Pilkington. Above the base, the framework of the wooden tower (29ft (8.8m) in height) was left open (i.e. not covered in weather boarding) and above that was the ogee-covered cap, making a total height of 70ft (21.3m). Smeaton was the first person to use cast iron in millwork, here in the form of a short windshaft with a cross attached, upon which the sails were mounted. The painting by Philip Reinagle (1749-1833) of the Calder Bridge, of which a small part only is reproduced here, is dated 1793. The mill, more Dutch in flavour and size than English, was demolished only about five years later.

Aberford North Mill
NGR SE 436 369

Some records for Aberford point to what was called a *Wind Oil Mill*, insured in 1782 for the sum of £800. The mill once standing to the north east of the village might originally have been used for pressing oil, but no further information on this has come to light. It was long used for conventional milling with four pairs of millstones, though it probably ceased work in the latter half of the nineteenth century. Subsequently it steadily deteriorated, culminating in its complete removal in the 1980s. One author, in 1902, speaking of rather different days, regarded the beautiful countryside round about as a "... hill and vale belvedere" but no mill tower dominates the area now.

This mill once possessed a mound around most of its lowest storey, but with a wood gallery probably completing the full circumference. A doorway eight feet wide gave access to the lowest level. The mound gave immediate access to the first floor and to the sails when they needed adjustment. A prominent string course, once the top of the tower, shows that a further storey had been added. The cast iron cross which held the sails is notable in the photograph.

Hessle Whiting Mill

NGR TA 022 254

Below: Built by Norman and Smithson sometime between 1806 and 1812, the whiting mill processed chalk from the large quarry at the southern limit of the Yorkshire Wolds. It continued in use by wind power (using roller sails) until 1925. Work was undertaken to preserve the mill in the 1980s and the tower still stands, now rather dwarfed by the northern tower of the Humber Bridge. It awaits restoration by the local council.

The two ladies in the photograph are Mrs and Miss Berkinshaw Cady. Mrs Berkinshaw Cady, in the wheelchair, died in 1904.

Hull, Stoneferry Mills

NGR TA 103 313 (oil mill)

NGR TA 103 312 (whiting mill)

Above: This picture shows the two mills which stood in adjacent premises at Stoneferry. The one on the left was an oil mill built in 1791 by the Hull millwrights Norman and Smithson, and was the first mill in the area to be fitted with Hooper's roller sails.

The one on the right was part of a whiting works. Along the chalk Wolds there were several quarries where the rock was extracted for engineering purposes but in some cases a small percentage of the output was crushed to produce whiting. The process involved crushing lumps of chalk in water, using edge runner millstones, and allowing the resultant slurry to overflow along a series of settling tanks, where the chalk in suspension gradually settled out according to size. The coarse material was used in paint whilst the finest went into toothpaste and cosmetics. This whiting mill was built in the 1780s and subsequently had the new roller sails fitted by Norman and Smithson.

In both these mills, the fantails shown in the picture were added sometime during the 1820s. The whiting mill almost certainly had a tail pole when built but it is probable the oil mill had an early type (horizontal) fantail.

The last remains of these structures disappeared in the 1960s.

Hull, Springbank Mill

NGR TA 090 293

Before the advent of synthetic dyes, a wide variety of natural materials were used to produce pigments for colouring paints and various other purposes. It was said of one paint maker that he "... made dull earths and mineral poisons to give out and yield up to him colours as rich as those of the solar rainbow." The paint maker concerned was Henry Blundell of Hull, who in 1811 founded the firm of Blundell and Spence. Their first factory was on Beverley Road in Hull, a site which included a five sail windmill, which they quickly adapted to drive machinery used to crush the raw materials.

The windmill had been built originally in 1788 as a corn mill, by James Norman. He was the son of a blacksmith who specialised in making anchors, but he also did more general work including repairs to at least one windmill. Millwrighting obviously appealed to James and he quickly acquired a reputation for quality work. In 1790 he went into partnership with Robert Smithson and immediately took out a licence for the supply of Hooper's Patent Roller Sails. This improved sail was widely used in Hull, Yorkshire and North Lincolnshire, where the firm built some very fine windmills, including several which contributed to the early industrialisation of Hull. They had their workshop close to the docks through which timber was imported and in later years widened their activities to include anything requiring the handling of large timbers, such as harbour and pier works. They continued in business until 1833.

Beverley Whiting Works

NGR TA 020 382

This mill was built in 1837 by Robert Garton, a millwright based in Beverley. Rather surprisingly in addition to the stones for crushing whiting, the mill was fitted up with three pairs of Derbyshire millstones. At this date such stones were unlikely to have been used for producing flour and it is quite possible they were used to provide feed for the numerous horses which must have been used to move material from the quarry to the mill and to deliver products to customers.

The truncated tower survives.

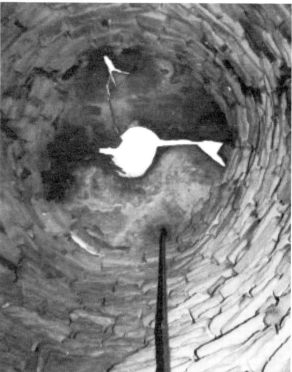

Pateley Bridge, Drayman's Field Quarry

NGR SE 166 658

Not far from the centre of Pateley Bridge, where Old Church Lane climbs steeply up to rough grass and gorse, is a large heap of stones. It is all that remains of a windmill used in the nineteenth century in connection with the sandstone quarrying activity nearby and in particular with Drayman's Field Quarry.

Before 2006, when the structure collapsed, it could be seen as a circular tower on a square base, built on to a steep incline. The circular tower was about 14ft (4.2m) high. The top had a circular capstone with a hole in its centre to locate an upright shaft, and a groove near its edge which served to locate some cap turning device. No machinery has remained, so what was its use? It seems unlikely to have been for pumping water from the quarry and if for cutting or dressing stone no evidence of their remains can be seen. The sails were said to be iron plates which could be heard clanging in Pateley Bridge far below.

There are hopes to rebuild the tower and, with this in mind, some courses of stone had already been carefully numbered and lettered.

Huddleston Grange

NGR SE 473 336

Of indeterminate age and with no obvious use in past days, a mill tower stands near Huddleston Grange, a property in a secluded position a little to the north of the Ledsham to Sherburn-in-Elmet road. The tower seems almost perched on the edge of the huge Huddleston Quarries, where stone has been extracted from mediaeval days to, among many places, York Minster. Again, the question asked of the Pateley Bridge mill can be asked here. What was the windmill used for? There was once a watermill only half a mile away. Huddleston was in a different setting from Pateley Bridge. It seems reasonable to assume that here was an example of an engine used to pump water out of the quarry workings, though it is apparent that it has been for long years out of commission.

A dense cover of trees and bushes largely hides the very rough stonework. The tower stands on an area of raised ground about 20ft (6m) above the approach road. There were originally three floors, with a total height of 20ft (6m). The internal diameter at ground level is 15ft (4.5m); thus the tower was a very small structure. A fireplace of some pretension is at ground level with its flue emerging outside higher up. The tower was once converted for use as a dovecote and was also crudely crenellated. The condition of the tower deteriorates and the embattling has gone, while the vegetation continues its stranglehold.

Hornsea Brickworks

NGR TA 201 464

One of the last mills to be built in the county, it was erected in 1865 by J A Woods to power his newly opened brickworks. Power was used for various purposes, first to drive a pug mill in which clay was crushed to the required consistency. It also powered a tramway incline which raised the raw materials from the pit. Additionally, it drove the pumps to de-water the clay pit. Wind power remained in use until the end of the nineteenth century.

The mill was probably demolished shortly after steam power was introduced in the early 1900s.

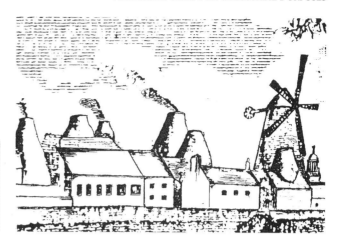

Leeds, Pottery Mill

NGR SE 304 322

Above & above right. After the oil mill in Wakefield, John Smeaton designed no more windmills until quite a number of years had passed by. The next windmill, called Sykefield Mill, built in the grounds of his house at Austhorpe in Leeds, was designed in 1772. It was used for oil pressing, as at Wakefield. In 1774 he constructed a mill in Leeds for grinding flints and colours for use in the pottery industry. This was the first of Smeaton's windmills in the country to have five sails. He judged this was the most efficient number for using the power of the wind. However, this could be inconvenient as, when one sail was damaged, the mill would need to cease work until it was replaced. With four-sailed mills the opposite sail to the damaged one could be removed and, it is said, about sixty per cent of the full energy is still available.

It is recorded that "On Sunday July 31st 1774, the sails of the windmill belonging to the Leeds Pottery fell down with a tremendous crash which, being looked on as a judgement for desecrating the Sabbath, the proprietors resolved that the mill should never be allowed to be worked afterwards on the Lord's Day." The mill continued in use by wind power until 1849 and the structure was eventually demolished about 1886.

Smeaton's windmill activities were continued with Chimney Mill (1781) and Stepney Mill (1783), both of Newcastle-on-Tyne, of which some much rebuilt parts of the former survive.

Morley, Haigh Moor

NGR SE 283 247

Right: This unusual but powerful wind engine stood on high land off Haigh Moor Road, south east of Morley. It was used for generating electricity for nearby Boyle Hall and dates from the closing years of the nineteenth century. The attached building housed the batteries. When the mill ceased its work the tower was demolished and the building was used as a slaughterhouse belonging to the Green family of butchers in the Morley area.

Hull, Eyre's Mill

NGR TA 123 309

Eyre's mill was one of a string of windmills which formerly stood along Holderness Road. Built in 1816, its claim to fame is its connection with Joseph Rank, the founder of the Rank milling empire. The mill was occupied by Rank's maternal grandparents and when Joseph's mother was about to give birth, as was often the case she went back to mum. Consequently Joseph was born in the cottage attached to the mill.

The premises have now been converted into a public house, the windmill being preserved externally as a feature. Having regard to the importance of the windmill to the industrial development of the city, the owners are to be congratulated for restoring and preserving this sole surviving example as a reminder of the once ubiquitous Hull windmill.

Leeds, Seacroft Mill

NGR SE 359 364

A newspaper report of 1767 told of a storm which had blown down a mill at Seacroft. If this is the mill in the photograph, and it was damaged rather than destroyed, perhaps it was the storm that necessitated the rebuilding or alterations at top level, evident in later years. There were two pairs of millstones once installed here and there was room for a third. A fireplace had a flue leading up through the walling to two external vents. For some years a shallow conical covering replaced the original cap.

When adjacent farm buildings were demolished in 1969 the tower, isolated by then, looked extremely fragile. Five years later, with a reinforced lining and twelve feet of the top again reconstructed, it was incorporated into a new hotel complex, now the Ramada Jarvis Hotel. After all these changes the tower now serves as a lounge at ground floor level, and has heating apparatus above. Fortunately at least something remains here to remind us of its story through the two hundred years or more of its life.

Riccall
NGR SE 617 374

Originally a typical East Yorkshire brick tower mill, dating from the second quarter of the nineteenth century, Riccall Mill continued in operation until the First World War. In 1911 it was purchased by a Mr Franklin who eventually converted it into a dwelling, where he lived until his death in 1934. The mill had a feature which was found in several windmills, namely a fire place at ground floor level, the flue from which passed upwards through the 18ins (0.5m) brickwork of the tower. Mrs Franklin is recorded as saying that the system was sufficient to warm the whole building in even the coldest weather.

In 1989 the property, by now in a poor state of repair, was acquired by Manolita Brage, who repaired the tower and converted the premises into a restaurant, adding a circular building around the ground floor of the tower to provide the necessary space. This has proved highly successful, offering excellent cuisine with all the friendly and personal service one finds with a family run business.

Scarborough Common
NGR TA 036 883

A post mill site of some antiquity which was replaced, in the mid 1780s, by a new tower built by Thomas Robinson. In an advertisement of 1829 it was described as being of five storeys in height. This is something of a puzzle as the present mill is seven storeys high and there is no obvious sign of the tower having been raised.

In the 1980s a dummy cap, sails and fantail were added and the mill is now part of a hotel. The mill is a prominent landmark in the town and would justify a more accurate cap, sails and fantail being provided.

Howden, Hail Mill

NGR SE 754 277

Below: Built by 1823, Hail Mill was a fine tower mill, well fitted out for a thriving business. An interesting feature was an elaborate internal cast iron support for the first floor. The mill was converted to a dwelling in the 1980s and can be seen to the north of the M62 motorway as one descends into East Yorkshire over the Ouse Bridge.

Burton Pidsea

NGR TA 244 309

Above: This quintessential East Yorkshire tower mill of five storeys was built in 1824 by the Hull millwrights, George and William Boyd. By 1872 the tenant miller was William Stephenson who ran the mill until his death in the 1890s, following which the business was carried on by his widow. In 1917 the freehold was purchased by Fred Stephenson who remained in possession until his death in 1945. It seems likely he ceased milling in the late 1930s and it is significant that during most of the period of his ownership, the property was continually in mortgage, an indication of the plight many millers experienced at this time. The mill still stands today and is used as part of a dwelling in conjunction with the original millhouse.

Keyingham New Mill

NGR TA 254 251

Left: Built in 1828, Keyingham New Mill had a lucky escape when struck by lightning on Good Friday 1897. The mill escaped serious damage but the lightning left its track, having peeled off all the paint on one side, from cap to the base, whilst the chain used for hauling up sacks of grain was fused into an "...unrecognisable mass". The mill has now been incorporated into a modern dwelling.

Follifoot

NGR SE 323 521

Right: On the north side of the road from Follifoot to Spacey Houses near Harrogate is a small settlement called Follifoot Ridge where a mill tower, long converted with extensions into a dwelling, is close to a former smithy, a tall square granary and what were once labourers' cottages. The dark millstone grit of the three storeyed building with decorative embattling is first mentioned in the nineteenth century, but by the end of that century it had already become a house.

Goole, Heron's Mill

NGR SE 750 237

Below and left: The prosperity of Goole quickly advanced after the docks were opened in 1826. From a population of about 300 at the turn of the century, it rapidly increased to reach 1700 by 1831. Two tower mills, both of which survive, were soon constructed for the needs of the town to replace Broadbent's Mill mentioned earlier.

The one, later called Heron's Mill, was a tower of six storeys, originally with a low access at a point outside the tower to permit easier loading and unloading of wagons at ground level. 45ft (13.7m) in height, it has its bricks laid horizontally rather than inclined with the batter of the walls, resulting in a stepped appearance to the brickwork.

By 1839 a 15hp steam engine had been installed, though work by wind only ceased in 1894. George Heron had bought the mill in 1870 and his family continued to work here. *Froment*, the wheat germ additive, was made in this mill until the whole business was sold by Roy Heron about 1975 and manufacture transferred to Timm's Mill. Now, with a three storeyed addition, it is part of a very substantial dwelling.

Leeds, Potternewton Mill
NGR SE 296 365

Below: One of the "... twin towers of Buslingthorpe" called *The Roundhouse* happily still survives. It is in Potternewton Mount on the north side of Leeds. Out of use as a mill by the middle of the nineteenth century it has been used as a dwelling for many years. With four storeys, strongly constructed in coursed stonework and with later additions of chimneys, external flues and a parapet at the top, the mill is a prominent landmark on Sugarwell Hill. In 1949 Mr and Mrs Bedford occupied the property. Mrs Bedford is recorded as saying "It's easy to clean, because there are no corners, and the thick walls make it cool in summer and warm in winter." Even a recent resident said she was thrilled with the experience of living in it. Though the appearance of the tower has changed greatly from its early days the structure just manages to retain a little of that rustic quality of the countryside once everywhere in this vicinity.

Kellington

NGR SE 546 242

Above: A magnesian limestone tower with brick dressings still stands at Kellington by the road from Knottingley. It had four floors with a domed cap and fantail, with a later auxiliary drive into the tower at low level. Wind power was used until the First World War after which it had a paraffin engine by Campbell of Halifax. All milling work had ceased by 1927. During World War II it was used as a Home Guard lookout post, later as living accommodation for eight years, then for trials with mushroom growing until it became derelict again. It was converted to a dwelling from about 1995.

Knottingley, King's Mill

NGR SE 487 235

Below: To the west of Knottingley's railway station in the area of Warren Avenue two windmills once stood next to each other. One of them was associated with the King's Mills, still a huge milling complex nearby and once worked by water power on the River Aire. The windmill would have acted as an additional resource in times of flood or drought. It is likely that this is the one which, after abandonment in 1848, was subsequently converted into a house. Certainly the three storey tower built of a rich red brick, gives the appearance of age, harking back to the latter part of the eighteenth century. In later years the railway company acquired the property for its employees. Its rustic appearance, in a setting of orchard and farm, and with its flower garden around it, allowed it to mature, said Miss Court and her sister Mrs Edith Rhodes, into "... a thing of beauty, a perfect setting on a summer evening". Its demolition in 1961, followed by housing development in the area, has changed the district for ever.

Kirkbymoorside

NGR SE 696 865

Above: This tower mill of six storeys was built for the Rivis family in 1839, at a cost of £1,000. It has now been converted into a dwelling.

Tollerton

NGR SE 514 638

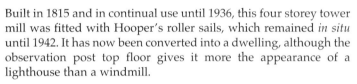

Built in 1815 and in continual use until 1936, this four storey tower mill was fitted with Hooper's roller sails, which remained *in situ* until 1942. It has now been converted into a dwelling, although the observation post top floor gives it more the appearance of a lighthouse than a windmill.

Morley, Drighlington

NGR SE 220 287

Empty windmill towers can have a variety of uses. There was an unusual one at Drighlington, where the tower was latterly used in an industrial process to recover wool from woollen rags with the aid of hydrochloric acid fumes. A similar process for the recovery of horsehair, for vacuum cleaner brushes, came later.

It has been claimed that the tower has some antiquity. Fifteen feet (4.6m) from the ground on a building alongside Moortop in Drighlington is an inscribed stone which reads -

This stone is taken from the old windmill which stood on this site for over 400 years - demolished 1949

Although there is no other evidence, the mill tower had on each side of the main entrance, the numbers 16 and 79, and it may be that 1679 was the date of building.

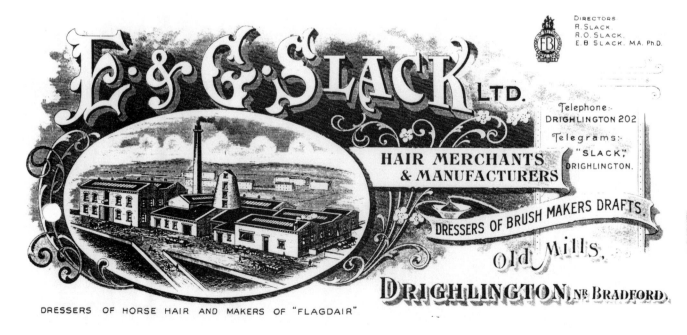

Yokefleet

NGR SE 821 237

The common use for empty mill towers was for agriculture. The mill at Yokefleet is a small early brick tower mill, in existence by 1780 and standing on the north bank of the River Ouse. When milling ceased, around 1860 it was thereafter used by a farmer for agricultural purposes. In the 1980s it provided a home for a large pig, but is now simply a general store.

As to what it may have stored in the past we can only guess. Yokefleet is a small hamlet, one of several located along the north bank of the River Ouse, close to its confluence with the River Trent, where the two rivers combine to form the Humber Estuary. As a result these hamlets had good links by water (inland and coastal) to much of England but were isolated so far as land access was concerned. Perhaps predictably, the local inhabitants were an independent lot. A stranger to the area in 1657 described them as "... crafty, false and very moorish to deal with." The Hope and Anchor Inn, a short distance downstream, had a notorious history of smuggling. Could the miller have concealed the odd sack of tobacco amongst the sacks of corn? Is it possible the sails of the windmill were left in a particular position to signal the presence of the Excise Men?

INDEX

Other mill sites with visible remains that are not included in this book.

Bisop Wilton	NGR	SE 795 550	Ruins of a small tower built in 1829.
Buckton		TA 180 715	Derelict shell of a tower mill.
Ellerton		SE 711 399	Part of a tower mill. Now used as a farm store.
Foston on the Wolds		TA 092 548	Ruins of a small tower mill built in 1820 to supplement the adjacent watermill.
Nafferton		TA 060 606	Derelict shell of a tower mill built in 1829.
South Duffield		SE 678 335	Derelict tower. Now used as a farm store.
Thornton-le-Clay		SE 677 656	Derelict shell of a small tower mill.
Waxholme		TA 326 292	Ruins of a tower mill.
Wressle		SE 710 312	Derelict tower built in 1827 to replace a post mill which was blown down in a storm. Now used as a farm store.
York, Haxby Road		SE 606 533	Minimal remains of a brick tower now incorporated into a modern dwelling.
York, Heworth Moor		SE 617 534	Shell of a pumping mill at the former brickworks.

The Authors

Laurence Turner

Laurence Turner has been interesteed in the study of windmills and watermills from his teenage days. His years in Yorkshire encouraged him to look at this area in greater depth. He is a retired Methodist minister who has served the Church mainly in the Leeds area, where he and his wife Pamela still live.

Roy Gregory

Roy Gregory's involvement with windmills began in 1974 when Skidby Windmill was placed in his care. This led to an absorbing interest in their history and conservation, in particular the work of the Hull millwrights, Messrs Norman and Smithson, and the use of windmills for industrial purposes. He is a retired solicitor and lives in Beverley.

This is a selection of useful titles and not a comprehensive bibliography.

Watts, M., *Windmills*, Shire Publications, 2006
(A good introduction to the subject)

Wailes, R., *The English Windmill*, Routledge & Kegan Paul, 1954
(Generally accepted as the leading book on the English windmill)

Gregory, R., *East Yorkshire Windmills*, Charles Skilton Ltd., 1985
(A detailed account of windmills in the eastern part of the county)

Harrison, J K., *Eight Centuries of Milling in North East Yorkshire*, North Yorkshire Moors National Park Authority, 2001
(A detailed account of both water and windmills in the north eastern part of the county)

Gregory, R., *The Industrial Windmill in Britain*, Phillimore & Co., 2005
(The reader will find a considerable amount of material relevant to developments in the county)

The principal organisation in England dealing with the conservation of wind, water and animal powered mills is the Mills Section of the Society for the Protection of Ancient Buildings. The Society offers advice and arranges courses on all matters relating to the repair and maintenance of mills. It also holds regular meetings and arranges annual visits to mills in different parts of the country. Membership is open to any person who has an interest in the subject. Enquires to The Mills Section, SPAB, 37 Spital Square, London, E1 6DY.

Acknowledgements

The authors are very glad to acknowledge the help that has been afforded in innumerable ways during the last thirty years or so. Thanks go especially to Robert Downing of Hatfield, who shared much information concerning Hatfield, Fishlake and Stainforth; to Kenneth Hartley of Selby, who wrote enthusiastically on mills of a wider area but especially for photographs of Skelton and West Cowick mills; to Richard Moody of Riccall, who, as a result of his local research, was able to provide photographs of Monk Fryston, East Cowick and Chapel Haddlesey mills, and to Dr J S Taylor of Thorne who likewise wrote extensively about mills of his locality. We thank John Goodchild of Wakefield who gave much help, but especially for his material of the Wakefield Soke MSS., and the Wakefield windmill in particular. Thanks also must be given to Eric Houlder of Pontefract, who provided the photograph of Darrington mill, and to Mr K E M Cline of Beverley who provided some very helpful information on sources relating to the windmills in East Yorkshire.

For individual mills, we warmly thank the following for their kindness and help: David Galloway (Airmyn), Stanley Robshaw and Arthur Bantoft (Barwick-in-Elmet), Noel Moxon (Cawthorne), Frank Glover and Mrs K Linley (Darrington), David Slack (Drighlington), Peter Aldred (Gildersome and Haigh Moor), Nigel Timm (Timm's Mill, Goole), Jack Wressell of Badsworth (Hatfield Woodhouse), Frank Waites (High Ackworth), Howard Woodall (Kippax), Ronald Gosney (Knottingley), Miss Cunningham of Kirk Smeaton (Little Smeaton), Mary Rogers of East Hardwick (Monk Fryston), H W Hartley of Carcroft, Doncaster (Moss), Dr Bob Gellatly (North Anston), Stan Beer, Eileen Burgess and Eric Stoyles (Pateley Bridge), Mr & Mrs T Wood and Rev C H Gardner (Dandy Mill, Pontefract), Mr J W Tonks of Castleford (St Thomas's Mill, Pontefract), Ruth Strong (Pudsey), Mrs B Robinson (Shelf), Miss E Thornton (Sherburn-in-Elmet), Harold Cowling and Gertrude Cowling (Swinefleet), Audrey Addy and Janet Threadgold (Sykehouse), John Pelling of Worthing (Bellwood's Mill, Thorne), Caroline Turner and Mr and Mrs Sharp (Ulleskelf), Susan Stones (Upton).

Other contributors to the study of mills must be added. With regard to the two towers at Wentworth, we are indebted to Arthur C Clayton, who wrote in detail on them in the *Transactions of the Hunter Archaeological Society vol. viii* (Sheffield 1963). The life and work of John Smeaton, and again with regard to the Wakefield windmill whose creation it was, was extensively covered by J Stephen Buckland in the *Proceedings of the Second Mill Research Conference* published by the Mills Research Group in 1984. We also include Mr H E S Simmons who not only investigated a vast number of mill sites in the 1940s throughout the country but also compiled in immense detail a huge amount of material concerning newspaper extracts, directories, bankruptcies and insurances. His work, held in the Library of the Science Museum, South Kensington, London, will always be invaluable to those who choose to study English windmills and watermills.

But we must especially acknowledge the help of John Harrison, who not only gave us the benefit of his extensive research into the mills of North East Yorkshire and allowed us to quote freely from his material, but also, in conjunction with his wife Ann, kindly read through a draft and made many helpful suggestions. However, we do of course accept full responsibility for any errors or omissions.